Books by David D. Wilson

A Study on the Holy Ghost
A Study on the Three Johns
The Revelation of Jesus Christ
A Study on the Warnings of Jude
A Study on the Two Peters

Order your copy at:

www.ParadiseGospelPress.com

or contact us at

Paradise Gospel Press
P.O. Box 184
Paradise, Texas 76073

The Revelation
of
Jesus Christ

Rev. David D. Wilson

PARADISE GOSPEL PRESS

THE REVELATION OF JESUS CHRIST, Wilson, David D.

First Edition

PARADISE GOSPEL PRESS

PARADISE GOSPEL PRESS

www.paradisegospelpress.com

ISBN: 978-1-946823-02-1

Dedication

I would like to dedicate this book to those who have supported me in my journey of writing and publishing the books that God has led me to complete.

First, my wife, Cynthia, for her support, encouragement and her help with deciphering my handwriting as well as my grammar.

Second, my brother-in-law, Farley Dunn of Three Skillet Publishing, for his encouragement, help, and walking me through the process to get to this point. Mr. Dunn was very instrumental in helping me get to the point of wanting my works published and remains a big help. Thank you again for all your help, Farley, because without you there would not be as many books as there are.

Finally, yet importantly, I want to thank my children and grandchildren for their understanding, encouragement and even giving me hints of which studies they wanted me to do next.

Table of Contents

Bibliography

Answers

Introduction

This writing is meant to be used as a Bible study. It is not in any way meant to be a reference book or commentary. I have tried, in this book, to bring forth a Bible study for lay members in the church, to open their eyes to some of the things that are going to happen in the coming future. Some commentaries are quoted verbatim, but as a rule most of the comments are mine. I don't agree with everything they've written, but as we all know, no two people agree on everything. The book of Revelation was written to the saints so that we will have some idea what the future holds, just before, during and after the tribulation period. Some people believe that after the tribulation the world will end, but that's not so. This world will continue for over a thousand years before the end. I'm amazed at some of the questions I've been asked, but it's simply because people don't understand what they read, or what they've been told. Please understand that the only "foolish" question is the question we don't ask. A question not asked is a question with no answer. It's been said, "But I don't know what to ask," and, "I'm afraid people will think that I'm dumb," or something along these lines. But, did you ever think that maybe they don't know either, and they are just like you, afraid to ask? A Bible study is just what it says, a study of the Bible, God's Holy Word. If we didn't study in school, then we wouldn't be able to read and write, to understand the world around us. So, we must do what? Study. In 2 Timothy 2:15, we read the following: *"Study to shew thyself approved unto God, a workman that needeth not to be ashamed, rightly dividing the word of truth."* So, to be doing God's will and work, we must study. I can truly agree with part of Richard Chichester's prayer to enable men and women ". . . to know Jesus Christ more clearly, to love him more dearly, and to follow him more nearly." I offer a few more scriptures for your consideration.

Deuteronomy 17:19

> *And it shall be with him, and he shall read therein all the days of his life: that he may learn to fear the LORD his God, to keep all the words of this law and these statutes, to do them:*

John 5:39

> *Search the scriptures; for in them ye think ye have eternal life: and they are they which testify of me.*

Acts 17:11

> *These were more noble than those in Thessalonica, in that they received the word with all readiness of mind, and searched the scriptures daily, whether those things were so.*

Romans 15:4

> *For whatsoever things were written aforetime were*

written for our learning, that we through patience and comfort of the scriptures might have hope.

As we go into the book of Revelation, we will do our best to answer a lot of your questions. But I will be the first to tell you, I don't have all the answers; no one does. For many, Revelation is a closed book. Preachers don't preach from it, and teachers don't teach it. In this study, we will do our best to open it up to you. The principle rule we will use is that "scripture must interpret scripture." For instance: Signified (sig-ni-fied) can be pronounced "sign-ified" to emphasize that much of the message is conveyed by symbols and signs. All this we will get into as we go through Revelation. It's my sincere hope and prayer that you will receive what God wants you to know. Enjoy the fact that God loves us enough to reveal His truth to our hearts. The warning is given; what we do with it is up to us.

Bro. David Wilson

The Revelation of Jesus Christ

Chapter 1

Revelation 1:1

The Revelation of Jesus Christ, which God gave unto him,
to shew unto his servants things which must shortly come
to pass; and he sent and signified it by his angel unto his
servant John:

The book of Revelation is a book that contains the revelation of Jesus Christ, which God gave to him for one specific purpose. What is that? To show unto his servant John things *"which must shortly come to pass."* **Revelation, despite what many people believe or say, is not the revelation of John.** The Word tells us point blank that the book of Revelation is the revelation of Jesus Christ. John was only the vessel that Jesus used to write the warning to the churches and to the saints of what the future holds for the world. To those who disbelieve Revelation, and there are many, I turn your attention to 2 Timothy 3:16-17. *"All scripture is given by inspiration of God, and is profitable for doctrine, for re-*

Note: In this study, all scripture is quoted from the *King James Version* unless otherwise stated. All scriptures are italicized.

proof, for correction, for instruction in righteousness: That the man of God may be perfect, thoroughly furnished unto all good works." Many people in our churches today pick and choose what scriptures they want to believe. But **the Word plainly states that all scripture is given by the inspiration of God.** There can be no picking and choosing; we must accept the whole Word of God. Another scripture to look at is 2 Timothy 4:1-2. "I charge thee therefore before God, and the Lord Jesus Christ, who shall judge the quick and the dead at his appearing and his kingdom; Preach the word; be instant in season, out of season; reprove, rebuke, exhort with all long-suffering and doctrine." Sadly to say, this shows us a picture of our modern-day churches, **turning from scripture and changing scripture to say what they want it to say.** They teach that under grace no one will miss heaven, that Jesus died for the whole world. Sin and sinners are welcomed into their churches. They ordain homosexuals as priest and pastors, something God's Word strictly forbids and condemns. I touch on these subjects to get them out of the way, so that we can keep our minds on Revelation. It's Jesus' Revelation, which God, His Father, gave to Him. Jesus then sent and signified it, by his angel, unto His servant John. Nowhere is John called the revelator.

Revelation 1:2

2 Who bare record of the word of God, and of the testimony of Jesus Christ, and of all things that he saw.

The testimony of John is that he remained true to his calling in Christ Jesus. The scripture states of John, "Who bare record of the word of God, and of the testimony of Jesus Christ, and of all things that he saw." This Revelation tells us of the things that will be taking place on the earth as well as things taking place in heaven **before, during and after the rapture of the saints or the church**.

Revelation 1:3

³ Blessed is he that readeth, and they that hear the words of this prophecy, and keep those things which are written therein: for the time is at hand.

Blessed are they – who? The people who read and hear the words of this prophecy and keep those things – what things? The things that are written in this book, because the time is at hand – what time is at hand? The soon return of our Lord Jesus Christ to take us, the saints, home to glory. **This book is a warning to the child of God and to the churches, to get as many saved as possible before Jesus comes back.** As we look at those around us who claim to be saved, we find that many of them had rather believe a lie than the truth. But it is only the truth that will set us free.

Revelation 1:4-8

⁴ John to the seven churches which are in Asia: Grace be unto you, and peace, from him which is, and which was, and which is to come; and from the seven Spirits which are before his throne;
⁵ And from Jesus Christ, who is the faithful witness, and the first begotten of the dead, and the prince of the kings of the earth. Unto him that loved us, and washed us from our sins in his own blood,

*⁶ And hath made us kings and priests unto God and his
Father; to him be glory and dominion for ever and ever.
Amen.
⁷ Behold, he cometh with clouds; and every eye shall see
him, and they also which pierced him: and all kindreds of
the earth shall wail because of him. Even so, Amen.
⁸ I am Alpha and Omega, the beginning and the ending,
saith the Lord, which is, and which was, and which is to
come, the Almighty.*

John begins to write to the seven churches which are in Asia. He begins with a greeting from our Lord and the seven Spirits which are before the throne. **John must have been well known to the churches**, because he simply states, *"John to the seven churches."* The seven Spirits denote the seven-fold ministry of the Holy Ghost. *"There is one Holy Ghost, but as the one candle holder has seven branches for seven candles, the Holy Ghost as the executive person of the Holy Trinity has seven ministry names, namely the Spirit of Adoption, the Spirit of Truth, the Spirit of Supplication, the Spirit of Glory, the Spirit of Holiness, the Spirit of Life, and the Spirit of Wisdom."* (Which denotes a seven-fold ministry with the emphasis being placed on the completeness of the Holy Ghost's ministry.) But **Jesus is the theme of Revelation**. He is given three titles, and they are: *Faithful Witness, First Begotten of the Dead* and *Ruler of the King of the Earth.* Then we see what Jesus has done for the church. Unto Him that loved us and washed us from our sins in His own blood. We are made kings and priests unto God. Be glory forever and ever.

Jesus is coming back. **The scripture says that He is coming** with clouds, every eye shall see Him, and all the people of the earth shall wail. **Jesus tells us who He is**: the Alpha and Omega, the beginning and the end, the Almighty.

Revelation 1:9-10

⁹ I John, who also am your brother, and companion in tribulation, and in the kingdom and patience of Jesus Christ, was in the isle that is called Patmos, for the word of God, and for the testimony of Jesus Christ.
¹⁰ I was in the Spirit on the Lord's day, and heard behind me a great voice, as of a trumpet,

In *Prevision of History*, by Rev. Elizabeth Williams, D. D., **John identifies himself without titles of honor or rank**; he simply calls himself brother and companion in tribulation, waiting in Christ Jesus. He names the place where he was the isle called Patmos, a small, barren island off the west coast of Asia Minor. He states that he is there for the Word of God and the testimony of Jesus Christ. According to Eusebius, an early church historian, John was banished or exiled to Patmos by the Roman Emperor Domitian in the year A.D. 95.

John further tells us that **he was in the spirit on the Lord's Day**. It simply should be accepted that John means that it was the first day of the week, what we call Sunday, the day of our Lord's resurrection.

Acts 20:7

⁷ And upon the first day of the week, when the disciples came together to break bread, Paul preached unto them, ready to depart on the morrow; and continued his speech until midnight.

17

1 Corinthians 16:2

² Upon the first day of the week let every one of you lay by him in store, as God hath prospered him, that there be no gatherings when I come.

John 20:19-20

¹⁹ Then the same day at evening, being the first day of the week, when the doors were shut where the disciples were assembled for fear of the Jews, came Jesus and stood in the midst, and saith unto them, Peace be unto you.
²⁰ And when he had so said, he shewed unto them his hands and his side. Then were the disciples glad, when they saw the Lord.

Revelation 1:11-20

¹¹ Saying, I am Alpha and Omega, the first and the last: and, What thou seest, write in a book, and send it unto the seven churches which are in Asia; unto Ephesus, and unto Smyrna, and unto Pergamos, and unto Thyatira, and unto Sardis, and unto Philadelphia, and unto Laodicea.
¹² And I turned to see the voice that spake with me. And being turned, I saw seven golden candlesticks;
¹³ And in the midst of the seven candlesticks one like unto the Son of man, clothed with a garment down to the foot, and girt about the paps with a golden girdle.
¹⁴ His head and his hairs were white like wool, as white as snow; and his eyes were as a flame of fire;
¹⁵ And his feet like unto fine brass, as if they burned in a

furnace; and his voice as the sound of many waters.
¹⁶ And he had in his right hand seven stars: and out of his mouth went a sharp twoedged sword: and his countenance was as the sun shineth in his strength.
¹⁷ And when I saw him, I fell at his feet as dead. And he laid his right hand upon me, saying unto me, Fear not; I am the first and the last:
¹⁸ I am he that liveth, and was dead; and, behold, I am alive for evermore, Amen; and have the keys of hell and of death.
¹⁹ Write the things which thou hast seen, and the things which are, and the things which shall be hereafter;
²⁰ The mystery of the seven stars which thou sawest in my right hand, and the seven golden candlesticks. The seven stars are the angels of the seven churches: and the seven candlesticks which thou sawest are the seven churches.

The great voice that John heard in Verse 10 is identified in Verse 11 of this chapter. Jesus tells us who He is by saying, "*I am Alpha and Omega, the first and the last.*" Then John is instructed that everything he is shown, he is to write in a book. Once it is written, **John is to send a copy to each of the seven churches which are in Asia.** Again, these seven churches are: Ephesus, Smyrna, Pergamos, Thyatira, Sardis, Philadelphia and Laodicea. In Verse 12, John turned to see the voice that spoke to him. John states that **he saw seven golden candlesticks, and in the midst of these candlesticks, John saw one like unto the Son of Man,** clothed with a garment down to His feet, having on a golden girdle. His head and His hair are white like wool, as white as snow. **In the Word of God, white denotes purity, without spot or stain, undefiled. It also speaks of wisdom and maturity, denot-**

ing the wisdom of the ages.

His eyes are like as a flame of fire. Here we see a simile describing the all-seeing, all-penetrating, all-knowing power of Jesus Christ. **This flame can burn out the dross in a life and at the same time warm the heart of the believer.** His feet are compared to fine brass, as if they burned in a furnace. **This symbolizes the power that enables Jesus to tread upon the enemy of our souls; nothing can bar or block His path.** His voice is as the sound of many waters. Have you ever stood next to a large waterfall? The sound is deafening. **This is like Jesus as He shows forth His power and glory. He commands and is obeyed.** In His right hand, He holds seven stars. Out of His mouth goes a sharp, two-edged sword. **The sword can be said to be the Word of God, and as Jesus speaks, His word is final.** As John sees this, he is overwhelmed and falls as one dead before the Lord.

The Lord reaches down, lays His right hand on John and tells him not to be afraid or fearful. Jesus reassures John of who He is by saying, *"I am the first and the last. I am he that liveth and was dead; and behold I am alive for evermore."* Jesus is telling John to remember when He walked with him, when He was crucified and when He rose from the dead. **He wants John to remember how they talked and preached God's Word.**

Again, Jesus tells John to write the things which he has seen, and the things that are and that are coming, for these things are warnings to the world and to His church to prepare for His return. The church is going to face trials and tribulations. For a long time, the church has been at ease, but things are changing. **Jesus tells us to fear not, for He is in control. These things must happen, but we are not to fear, for our trust is in Jesus Christ, our Savior.**

Jesus tells John that the seven stars which he saw in Jesus' right hand are the angels of the seven churches. As we look at this mystery, John wasn't writing to angels from heaven, but to the pastors of the seven churches, **those who were responsible for the preaching of the gospel and keeping the churches in line with God's Word**. The seven golden candlesticks are represented as the seven churches in Asia. We can truly say that these seven churches were the most influential churches of that time. They were larger and more active in the ministry of the gospel than any others.

There's a problem when studying the book of Revelation. Many people look at these scriptures and say they don't understand what they are reading. How do we know what's what? Some have said, "I don't read it because it scares me." The book of Revelation must be studied with much prayer. Some scriptures are written as fact, to be taken just as they are written, and some as symbolism, such as the angels of the churches, who are the pastors. Other scriptures are parenthetical. As a rule, most people want everything laid out for them. However, **when it comes to God's Word, there are times when we must dig out what God wants us to know**. The book of Revelation is a picture of the near future; the coming future of mankind. **We cannot be like many people and hide our heads in the sand. Jesus loves us enough to give us warning. Use it, and let it make you a better person.**

Chapter 1 Review Questions

1. Whose Revelation is it?

_____

2. This book is a

_____

3. To whom does John write?

_____

_____

4. How many titles is Jesus given here?

_____

_____

5. What island was John on and why?

_____

_____

6. To whom did John write this book?

_____

_____

7. Who are the Angels of the Churches?

_____

_____

8. Name the seven churches.

_____

_____

_____

_____

_____

_____

9. What was the Son of Man in the midst of?

_____

_____

Chapter 2

The Seven Churches

The letters we are about to look at and discuss are to the seven churches of Asia. These churches are located in Ephesus, Smyrna, Pergamos, Thyatira, Sardis, Philadelphia, and Laodicea. As we look at these churches, we will also see that **they represent the seven church ages**. These ages divide the period of time from Christ's death on the cross to this present day. They define some of the problems that the churches throughout the ages have faced and gone through, and that we face today. The following diagram illustrates the church ages:

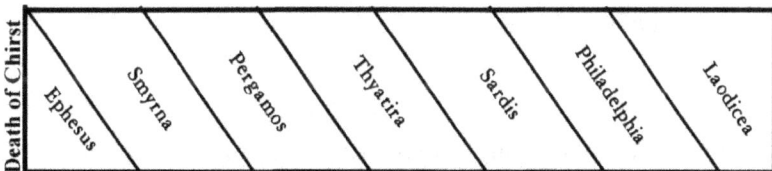

Prevision of History states: "About one-eighth of the book of Revelation is devoted to the messages to the seven churches." These messages should not be passed over lightly, because they deal with the now, this present age. **There are lessons here that we must learn, if we are to come through victorious in our service of the Lord.** Seven times we will read these words: *"He*

that hath an ear, let him hear what the spirit saith unto the churches." The Lord is trying to get our attention, and we don't seem to be listening.

Unto the Church of Ephesus

Ephesus, during this time, was one of the largest cities in Asia Minor, and one of the largest in the Roman Empire. The city is said to have had about 500,000 people. It's hard for me to envision a city so large in this period in history. We must remember that the only means of travel was on foot, horseback or by cart or wagon. What a place Ephesus must have been with its open-air markets and bazaars, and no modern-day conveniences! People of today would consider it unbearable. But Ephesus was one of the most modern cities of its time. **In Ephesus, there was a strong church in its beginnings, but the devil was fighting and bringing in false doctrines, as we shall see.** As a center of population, there was, in Ephesus, all manner of false gods and their temples, although that's not the purpose of this study.

The worship of Diana was one of the main religions; the temple of Diana at Ephesus was considered one of the seven wonders of the ancient world. Diana (in Greece she was known as Artemis) was the Roman goddess of the hunt, the moon and birthing. This means she brought favor to those who worshipped her in their hunting, and she gave them light as well as protected the women when it came time to deliver the babies. **Being involved with childbirth expanded to the temples as well, as the priestesses were used for prostitution.**

This was the temple to which Paul referred in Acts 19:26. *"Moreover ye see and hear, that not alone at Ephesus, but almost throughout all Asia, this Paul hath persuaded and turned away much people, saying that they be no gods, which are made with hands:"* There were hundreds, maybe thousands of priests working in Diana's Temple, along with the priestesses who were dedicated to prostitution in the temple service.

Revelation 2:1-7

[1] Unto the angel of the church of Ephesus write; These things saith he that holdeth the seven stars in his right hand, who walketh in the midst of the seven golden candlesticks;
[2] I know thy works, and thy labour, and thy patience, and how thou canst not bear them which are evil: and thou hast tried them which say they are apostles, and are not, and hast found them liars:
[3] And hast borne, and hast patience, and for my name's sake hast laboured, and hast not fainted.
[4] Nevertheless I have somewhat against thee, because thou hast left thy first love.
[5] Remember therefore from whence thou art fallen, and repent, and do the first works; or else I will come unto thee quickly, and will remove thy candlestick out of his place, except thou repent.
[6] But this thou hast, that thou hatest the deeds of the Nicolaitans, which I also hate.
[7] He that hath an ear, let him hear what the Spirit saith unto the churches; To him that overcometh will I give to eat of the tree of life, which is in the midst of the paradise of God.

This letter, like the other six to come, begins the same

way: *"Unto the church of Ephesus write."* In Chapter One we read, *"to write to the angel of the churches,"* but in these opening lines, we see that **the letter, though addressed to the angel or pastor, is to the whole church body**. Jesus begins by telling everyone who He is, the one who holds the seven stars in His right hand and that *"walketh in the midst of the seven golden candlesticks."* There's no wondering as to who's speaking, Jesus Christ, the Lord of lords, and the King of kings. Jesus tells the church, *"I know thy works, and thy labor, thy patience."* He knows their hearts, how they tried the spirits and found some to be liars. Then the dreaded words come: *"Nevertheless I have somewhat against thee, because thou hast left thy first love."*

Do you remember your first love? Do you remember their name, how they looked; how pretty she was or how handsome he was? How your heart kind of skipped a beat? These are things that are usually imprinted upon our minds and that we never forget, no matter how old we get. I don't know why, it just seems to work that way for everyone, boy or girl.

This is how it is when we meet Jesus Christ for the first time. No matter what happens or comes our way, the point of our salvation is imprinted upon our heart and mind. You can ask any Christian, and they will tell you they remember when they first got saved. They may not remember the exact day or time, but they can tell you how they felt when Jesus changed their lives forever. We will never forget that experience. A person can walk away from their salvation, but they will never forget it.

How many, not just saints, but also churches, do we know that have left their first love? Churches that teach and condone sin and bring it into their assemblies, condoning same sex marriages, and ordaining ministers and pastors who are practicing homosexuals, things that God's Word strictly forbids. **Sometimes we**

wonder how far down God will let us go; but be sure of this one thing, there is a stopping place, and we are almost there.

The Ephesians were told to remember from where they had fallen. Remember. It does us good sometimes to remember where we were when the Lord saved us, and where we could have been today had it not been for the Lord's saving grace. The message was to **repent, to go back to serving the Lord the way we did when we first felt the saving power of our Lord**. The Ephesians were told that if they didn't repent, that Jesus would come quickly and remove them as one of the leading churches. There was one thing in their favor, that they hated the works of the Nicolaitanes. The Nicolaitanes were a sect of people who called themselves Christians, yet were anything but. They had evil practices and loose morals much like the modern church of today. Finis Jennings Dake states that the Nicolaitanes were "Followers of Nicolaus, a heretic. They are supposed to have been a sect of Gnostics who practiced and taught impure and immoral doctrines, such as the community of wives, that committing adultery and fornication was not sinful, and that eating meats offered to idols was lawful."

According to Wikipedia, Gnostics are people who use a form of philosophy that says the physical world should be shunned, and the spiritual world (God's world) should be embraced. The **Gnostic ideas influenced many ancient religions** which teach that gnosis (being interpreted as knowledge, enlightenment, salvation, emancipation or "oneness with God") may be reached by practicing philanthropy to the point of personal poverty, sexual abstinence and diligently searching for wisdom by helping others. To put it in simple, plain words, you get to heaven through your works, and if you don't do enough, you won't make it to heaven.

"He that hath an ear, let him hear what the Spirit saith unto the churches:" Jesus closed this letter with a promise to the church. *"To him that overcometh will I give to eat of the tree of life which is in the midst of the paradise of God."* **What greater promise can be given than to eat of the tree of life in the paradise of God than to dwell with our Lord forever and ever?** Are we listening to "thus sayeth the Lord," or are we living every day as if it was our last? Do we walk in the footsteps of Jesus, and do we spread the gospel message? He that hath an ear let him hear.

Unto the Church of Smyrna

Revelation 2:8-11

8 And unto the angel of the church in Smyrna write; These things saith the first and the last, which was dead, and is alive;
9 I know thy works, and tribulation, and poverty, (but thou art rich) and I know the blasphemy of them which say they are Jews, and are not, but are the synagogue of Satan.
10 Fear none of those things which thou shalt suffer: behold, the devil shall cast some of you into prison, that ye may be tried; and ye shall have tribulation ten days: be thou faithful unto death, and I will give thee a crown of life.
11 He that hath an ear, let him hear what the Spirit saith unto the churches; He that overcometh shall not be hurt of the second death.

John writes unto the angel of the church, or pastor, of the church in Smyrna. Again, Jesus tells the church who He is, that

He is *"the first and the last, which was dead, and is alive."* **There can be no mistake about who Jesus is.** He makes it very plain. The Lord begins by telling them that He knows their works, their tribulations and also their poverty.

Jesus knows their works, what they have done for the Lord, in working for the church, their witnessing, their faithfulness, their reaching out to those around them. Sometimes simply living a good Christian life speaks much louder than anything that we could say. How do we respond to unfavorable circumstances? Do we get mad easily; are we honest in our dealings with others?

Jesus knows what tribulations we go through, the tests and the trials of this life. Jesus knows what the devil does to us through those who are around us. Jesus knows that Satan desires to sift us as a grain of wheat. Our Lord and Savior trod this world before us, and He came through victorious over all the tricks of the enemy. Jesus did it and tells us we can too, if we will put our faith in Him.

Jesus knows our poverty and distresses, yet at the same time, He tells us that we are rich, rich in the blessings of a loving God. We have a Savior who opened up the doors of heaven for us. All that our heavenly Father has is ours, if we will trust and believe on Him. The world hates us because it hated Jesus before us. However, Jesus tells us to not be afraid, to not let ourselves be overtaken by fear. For greater is He that is in me than he that is in the world. (John10:29)

Jesus tells them that He knows the works of those who profess to be Jews and are lying; there is a great deal of difference between those who profess and those who actually possess the power and glory of the Lord in their souls. Next Jesus gives them words of hope and tells them not to fear that which is to come upon them. All their suffering will not be in vain. What suffering?

The suffering that the world is about to thrust upon them. Some, the devil will cast into prison that their faith may be tried.

These people will go through tribulations, but are told to be faithful unto death. They shall receive a crown of life. *"He that hath an ear, let him hear what the Spirit saith unto the churches."* Again, a promise to the saints, *"He that overcometh shall not be hurt of the second death."* What a great promise to believers. I hope you also noticed that **there was no rebuke to this church for any wrongdoing.** This was a church where the Lord was master and He was in control. This is the type of church that wins the victory over sin. Pray that God gives us these types of churches, where **truth is preached and lives are changed**. Saints, our victory can only be in Jesus Christ our Lord. Praise to our most high God.

Unto the Church of Pergamos

Revelation 2:12-17

[12] And to the angel of the church in Pergamos write; These things saith he which hath the sharp sword with two edges;
[13] I know thy works, and where thou dwellest, even where Satan's seat is: and thou holdest fast my name, and hast not denied my faith, even in those days wherein Antipas was my faithful martyr, who was slain among you, where Satan dwelleth.
[14] But I have a few things against thee, because thou hast there them that hold the doctrine of Balaam, who taught Balac to cast a stumblingblock before the children of Israel, to eat things sacrificed unto idols, and to commit

fornication.

[15] So hast thou also them that hold the doctrine of the Nicolaitans, which thing I hate.

[16] Repent; or else I will come unto thee quickly, and will fight against them with the sword of my mouth.

[17] He that hath an ear, let him hear what the Spirit saith unto the churches; To him that overcometh will I give to eat of the hidden manna, and will give him a white stone, and in the stone a new name written, which no man knoweth saving he that receiveth it.

In Verse 13, **the Word talks about where Satan lives and sits or rules.** This is talking about a sect that was dedicated to the worship of Satan which was located in Babylon at that time. This is what it means when it talks about God knowing where Satan dwelled.

Pergamos, like the other cities, was a center of commerce, a city of diverse people and the worship of many gods. The Christian church in Pergamos was a church of compromise. Instead of holding true to the gospel teaching, it was easier to let false doctrines into the church, than to take a stand against the devil and doctrines of demons. This is exactly what's happening to the church today. **Instead of facing the enemy and standing up for the truth of God's Word, the Church crumbles before criticism and the rebuke of sinners,** and changes its belief and doctrine to try to keep from being called into the limelight. As for the Bible-believing church where the truth of God is still taught and preached, it is still held most precious.

The message to the Pergamos church starts with the familiar words, *"And to the angel of the church write."* The Word then leads us into the introduction of Jesus as He identifies Himself.

"These things saith He which hath the sharp sword with two edges." This sword is the gospel of Jesus Christ the final authority, God's Holy Word by which all men will be judged. Jesus lays out the charges against the church. *"I know thy works, and where thou dwellest, even where Satan's seat is:"* Jesus then begins to tell the church that He also knows its good points: Also some in the church still hold fast to the name of Jesus and have not denied the faith that was delivered unto them at salvation, even in the days of persecution when Antipas was martyred for his standing up for the truth of God's Word. **How vicious people can be when you stand for the truth and by so doing point out their sin and ungodliness.** Their wrath has no bounds; they have no mercy. When they know they are wrong, they say they are right and will destroy anyone who disagrees. And the church still compromises. Jesus goes so far as to even tell the church where Antipas was slain, where Satan dwelt. Further condemnation follows as Jesus begins to tell the church, *"But I have a few things against thee, because thou hast there them that hold the doctrine of Balaam."* Some of their deeds were to eat the things sacrificed unto idols, and committing fornication. There were also in the church those that espoused the doctrine of the Nicolaitans, which Jesus says, *"Which thing I hate."* Again, very little is known about the beliefs of the Nicolaitans, but whatever it was, Jesus hated it. **The warning is given:** *repent* **or else.** Jesus will come quickly to fight against the purveyors or providers of evil. *"He that hath an ear, let him hear what the spirit saith unto the churches."*

The promise to overcomers is that He will give to eat of the hidden manna, they will receive a white stone, and **in the stone a new name will be written which no one knows saving he that received it.** The white stone signifies white for purity and the precious Word of God. The new name isn't much understood, but possibly we, the bride, after the marriage, will take the name of our Lord and Savior.

Unto the Church of Thyatira

In *Prevision of History,* "Thyatira was a commercial city of importance, it was situated east and a little south of Pergamos. Thyatira was known for its trade guilds. The city was devoted to the worship of Apollo." The trade guilds all had their own patron gods; everything in Thyatira was linked to pagan ritual and worship. In this environment, the Christian church had to struggle and combat the devil on every side. Here in America, the true church is struggling every day. We are not fighting against the same kind of pagan religions. But **we fight the same devil, we fight modernism, we fight complacent spirits, spirits of unconcern, we fight compromise, sin is rampant among people who call themselves Christians and false doctrines prevail in our churches.**

Revelation 2:18-29

[18] And unto the angel of the church in Thyatira write; These things saith the Son of God, who hath his eyes like unto a flame of fire, and his feet are like fine brass;
[19] I know thy works, and charity, and service, and faith, and thy patience, and thy works; and the last to be more than the first.
[20] Notwithstanding I have a few things against thee, because thou sufferest that woman Jezebel, which calleth herself a prophetess, to teach and to seduce my servants to commit fornication, and to eat things sacrificed unto idols.

*21 And I gave her space to repent of her fornication; and
she repented not.*

*22 Behold, I will cast her into a bed, and them that commit
adultery with her into great tribulation, except they repent
of their deeds.*

*23 And I will kill her children with death; and all the
churches shall know that I am he which searcheth the
reins and hearts: and I will give unto every one of you
according to your works.*

*24 But unto you I say, and unto the rest in Thyatira, as
many as have not this doctrine, and which have not known
the depths of Satan, as they speak; I will put upon you
none other burden.*

25 But that which ye have already hold fast till I come.

*26 And he that overcometh, and keepeth my works unto the
end, to him will I give power over the nations:*

*27 And he shall rule them with a rod of iron; as the vessels
of a potter shall they be broken to shivers: even as I
received of my Father.*

28 And I will give him the morning star.

*29 He that hath an ear, let him hear what the Spirit saith
unto the churches.*

This letter, like the other three, starts out the same way: *"And unto the angel of the church in Thyatira write."* Stop for a minute and think what this pastor must have thought when he opened the letter and read its contents. How his heart must have felt as the impact of what he was reading struck home. Church, we are no different from the churches that we're reading about. Look around you, use your spiritual eyes to see the very same happenings in the so-called church world; but God hasn't given us just one letter to learn by, but **He has given us seven letters as a warning to the church world, and still she doesn't listen**.

What will it take? Can anything wake the church world? In the introduction, *"These things saith the Son of God, who hath his eyes like unto a flame of fire, and his feet are like fine brass:"* (the underlining is mine), Jesus is trying to get our attention. **He's giving a picture of Himself as the eternal Son of God.** What will it take? Our Lord confirms that He knows these people's works, and in Verse 19 states, *"I know thy works, and charity, and service, and faith, and thy patience, and thy works; and the last be more than the first."* All these things speak very well for the church, but as good as this sounds, **there's still failure in the midst of God's church**.

The hammer drops as Jesus tells the Church, I have a few things against thee. Number one: *"thou sufferest that woman Jezebel, who calls herself a prophetess to teach and to seduce my servants to commit fornication, to eat things sacrificed to idols."* Jesus further states, *"I gave her space to repent and she repented not."* If they don't repent, they shall be put into great tribulation, except they repent of their deeds. The Lord goes on because of this great sin, and He states, *"I will kill her children with death,"* and all the churches shall know who He is. He is *"He that searcheth the reins and heart."* This promise He also gives, *"I will give unto everyone of you according to your work."* When we really stop to think about what's being said, **God doesn't send a soul to hell. We send ourselves there** by the things we say, think and do that's not like unto God. The fault lies at our door. We cannot really blame anyone but ourselves. The Lord again speaks to all those who don't hold to the doctrine that was described, those who have not known the depths of Satan, that He would not put upon them any other burden.

"But that which ye have already hold fast till I come." The promise to the Christians at Thyatira is to *"he that overcometh, and keepeth my works unto the end, to him will I give power over the nations: And he shall rule them with a rod of iron; as the vessels of a potter shall they be broken to shivers: even as I received of my Father. And I will give him the morning star. He that hath an ear, let him hear what the Spirit saith unto the churches."*

We have the promise that **if we will serve the Lord and hold fast to His Word, that we will rule and reign with Him.** All who overcome and live for the Lord will one day see Him as He is, the bright and morning star, the Lily of the Valley, the Rose of Sharon, The Holy Son of God, Jesus our Redeemer, our Savior, our soon coming King.

Chapter 2 Review Questions

1. Name the seven churches of Asia.

_____

_____

_____

_____

_____

_____

2. What do the seven churches represent?

_____

_____

3. The church of Ephesus had left what?

_____

4. What promise does the Lord close the letter with?

_____

_____

5. In every letter Jesus tells the church who He is. In the letter to Smyrna, who does Jesus say He is?

_____

_____

6. What promise is given to the Smyrna church?

_____

_____

_____

7. Why was Antipas martyred?

_____

_____

_____

8. What was the promise given to the church at Thyatira?

_____

_____

_____

Chapter 3

Unto the Church of Sardis

Revelation 3:1-6

[1] And unto the angel of the church in Sardis write; These things saith he that hath the seven Spirits of God, and the seven stars; I know thy works, that thou hast a name that thou livest, and art dead.
[2] Be watchful, and strengthen the things which remain, that are ready to die: for I have not found thy works perfect before God.
[3] Remember therefore how thou hast received and heard, and hold fast, and repent. If therefore thou shalt not watch, I will come on thee as a thief, and thou shalt not know what hour I will come upon thee.
[4] Thou hast a few names even in Sardis which have not defiled their garments; and they shall walk with me in white: for they are worthy.
[5] He that overcometh, the same shall be clothed in white raiment; and I will not blot out his name out of the book of life, but I will confess his name before my Father, and before his angels.
[6] He that hath an ear, let him hear what the Spirit saith

unto the churches.

"*And unto the angel of the Church in Sardis write,*" repeating as before, that the letter is written to the pastor of the church. But the letter wasn't only to the pastor; **it was for the whole church**. The whole church stood at fault for permitting the devil to compromise the gospel; "*these things saith he that hath the seven Spirits of God, and the seven stars.*" We know by the words of Jesus that the seven stars are the angels or pastors of the churches. The seven spirits point to the perfection of the work of the Holy Ghost. In *Prevision of History*, which covers both Daniel and Revelation, by Elizabeth Williams, D.D., Dr. Williams states: "There is one Holy Ghost, but as the one candle holder has seven branches for seven candles, the Holy Ghost as the executive person of the Holy Trinity has seven ministry names, namely: **Spirit of Adoption** [Romans 8:15-16 – *15 For ye have not received the spirit of bondage again to fear; but ye have received the Spirit of adoption, whereby we cry, Abba, Father. 16 The Spirit itself beareth witness with our spirit, that we are the children of God:*], **Spirit of Truth** [John 14:17 – *Even the Spirit of truth; whom the world cannot receive, because it seeth him not, neither knoweth him: but ye know him; for he dwelleth with you, and shall be in you. & John 15:26 – But when the Comforter is come, whom I will send unto you from the Father, even the Spirit of truth, which proceedeth from the Father, he shall testify of me:*], **Spirit of Supplication** [Ephesians 6:18 – *Praying always with all prayer and supplication in the Spirit, and watching thereunto with all perseverance and supplication for all saints;*], **Spirit of Glory** [1 Peter 4:13 – *But rejoice, inasmuch as ye are partakers of Christ's sufferings; that, when his glory shall be revealed, ye may be glad also with exceeding joy.*], **Spirit of Holiness** [Romans 1:4 – *And* *declared to be the Son of God with power, according to the spirit of holiness, by the resurrection from the dead:*], **Spirit of Life** [Revelation 11:11 – *And after three days and an half the Spirit of life from God entered into them, and they stood upon their feet; and great fear fell upon them which saw them.*], **Spirit of Wisdom** [Ephesians 1:17 – *That the God of our Lord Jesus Christ, the Father of glory, may give unto you the spirit of wisdom and revelation in the knowledge of him:*] (which in turn denotes a sevenfold ministry). The completeness of the Holy Ghost's ministry is the emphasis."

Jesus, again, emphasizes, *"I know thy works, that thou hast a name that thou livest and art dead."* How can a person be alive and dead at the same time? **Before we were saved, we woke up each morning alive but at the same time dead spiritually.** Jesus spoke of knowing their works, that they had a name. There are denominations even today that teach that salvation comes through works. Sadly, they are wrong; we need to show forth works, but **we are saved by grace through the shed blood of Jesus**. The Sardis church was told to be watchful and to strengthen their spiritual lives, which were ready to die. Warning: *"I have not found your works perfect before God."* The Church is told to remember what they first received and heard, to repent and to hold fast. The same warning is ringing throughout the land today. If the church doesn't watch and prepare, Jesus will come as a thief, in an hour that they think not, and bring judgment. **The promise of the Lord then comes to the faithful.** There are a few that have not defiled themselves, and they shall walk with Him in white, for they are worthy. A message for us today: *"He that overcometh, the same shall be clothed in white raiment; and I will not blot out his name out of the Book of Life, but I will confess his name before my Father, and before His angels."* What a promise, what a future to work for, to be with Jesus, the one who died for us, He who loved us, when we were unlovable. He that hath an ear, let him hear what the spirit saith unto the churches.

Unto the Church of Philadelphia

Revelation 3:7-13

[7] And to the angel of the church in Philadelphia write; These things saith he that is holy, he that is true, he that hath the key of David, he that openeth, and no man shutteth; and shutteth, and no man openeth;
[8] I know thy works: behold, I have set before thee an open door, and no man can shut it: for thou hast a little strength, and hast kept my word, and hast not denied my name.
[9] Behold, I will make them of the synagogue of Satan, which say they are Jews, and are not, but do lie; behold, I will make them to come and worship before thy feet, and to know that I have loved thee.
[10] Because thou hast kept the word of my patience, I also will keep thee from the hour of temptation, which shall come upon all the world, to try them that dwell upon the earth.
[11] Behold, I come quickly: hold that fast which thou hast, that no man take thy crown.
[12] Him that overcometh will I make a pillar in the temple of my God, and he shall go no more out: and I will write upon him the name of my God, and the name of the city of my God, which is new Jerusalem, which cometh down out of heaven from my God: and I will write upon him my new

name.
[13] He that hath an ear, let him hear what the Spirit saith
unto the churches.

The church at Philadelphia is sometimes called the revival church. It, in the period of the church ages, shows a time of revival in the churches. It's argued that this church age is coming to a close, and we are now entering the Laodicean church age. I must agree with this train of thought, but **all that is in me hopes for one more great revival to spread across the world calling people to God.** The salutation to the Philadelphia church begins as the others: *"And to the angel of the church in Philadelphia write."* Just think what preachers (pastors) would do if they received such letters today. I believe that ninety to ninety-five percent would call it a hoax and throw the letter away. They simply don't believe that God would treat them in such a way. Their self-importance would demand that Jesus come and speak to them personally. **Too many of our leading ministers think everybody should look up to them and give them the honor they deserve.** Not long ago I was reading that one of these preachers' wives was flying someplace. She didn't get the treatment she thought she deserved, and in a haughty spirit, she commented to the steward, "Don't you know who I am?" The most important man that has ever lived was humble, kind, compassionate and loving to everyone. Who do we think we are? **We're not better than our Master, and never will be.** Next, we see the characteristics of Christ put forth. *"These things saith He that is holy, He that is true, He that hath the key of David, He that openeth, and no man shutteth, and shutteth, and no man openeth."* Jesus declares Himself to be Holy, [1 Peter 1:14-15 – *[14] As obedient children, not fashioning yourselves according to the former lusts in your ignorance: [15] But* *as he which hath called you is holy, so be ye holy in all manner of conversation;*] Because it is written, *"Be ye holy; For I am Holy."* [Hebrews 12:14 – *Follow peace with all men, and holiness, without which no man shall see the Lord:*] Scripture states very plainly that for us to see Jesus, we must live in the holiness of our Lord. This leaves a lot of the so-called Christians in the cold. Why is revival so important? To get the church ready for the rapture. [2 Chronicles 7:14 – *If my people, which are called by my name, shall humble themselves, and pray, and seek my face, and turn from their wicked ways; then will I hear from heaven, and will forgive their sin, and will heal their land.*] In this scripture, God says, *"If my people which are called by my name, shall humble themselves, and pray, and seek my face, and turn from their wicked ways."* This is the message Jesus is trying to get across to the church: **If you want to go to heaven, you must turn from your wicked ways.**

Jesus continues to say, *"I know thy works; behold I have set before thee an open door, and no man can shut it; for thou hast a little strength, and hast kept my word, and hast not denied my name."* What praise Jesus gives to His people! Because of their stand, Jesus opened the door of revival. In *Studies in Revelation,* by J. Narver Gortner, published in 1948, Bro. Gortner states that the church ages overlap, which is something that I also believe. So, the Philadelphian period overlaps into the Laodicean period, and it's the Philadelphian church that will be raptured out of this world when Jesus comes. In fact, we are living in the Laodicean period now, but that's no excuse to belong to the Laodicean church. Those who make the rapture most surely will come out of the Philadelphian church. But Jesus still gives the Laodiceans a chance if they repent. **Even after the rapture of the saints, if those who are left will give their lives for Jesus' sake and the**

gospel, there's a chance. Our Lord's promise still goes on: *"Because thou hast kept the word of my patience, I also will keep thee from the hour of temptation, which shall come upon the entire world, to try them that dwell upon the earth."* **What better way to keep us from the hour of temptation than for the rapture to take us home to be with Him?**

" 'Behold I come quickly:' hold fast, let no man take your crown. To the over comers they shall be made pillars in the temple of God." Jesus again warns that He will come quickly. **Scripture says that in a moment, in the twinkling of an eye, we will be caught up to meet Jesus in the air, and so shall we ever be with Jesus.** Wherever Jesus is, there we will be also. [1 Thessalonians 4:13-18 – *13 But I would not have you to be ignorant, brethren, concerning them which are asleep, that ye sorrow not, even as others which have no hope. 14 For if we believe that Jesus died and rose again, even so them also which sleep in Jesus will God bring with him. 15 For this we say unto you by the word of the Lord, that we which are alive and remain unto the coming of the Lord shall not prevent them which are asleep. 16 For the Lord himself shall descend from heaven with a shout, with the voice of the archangel, and with the trump of God: and the dead in Christ shall rise first: 17 Then we which are alive and remain shall be caught up together with them in the clouds, to meet the Lord in the air: and so shall we ever be with the Lord. 18 Wherefore comfort one another with these words.*] **Hallelujah, are you ready, are you looking for Jesus to return?** Do you wonder what it will be like? I do. I want to see my loved ones gone on before, Mother, Dad, Son, but most of all, I want to see Jesus more than anything.

The Philadelphian church is the raptured church. Jesus will write upon them the name of God and the name of the city of God which is New Jerusalem. He will write upon the raptured His name. Bro. Gortner, in *Studies in Revelation,* writes, "When a man weds a woman he gives to that woman his own name and our Lord is going to give His name, His new name, to His bride." Church, we are the bride of Christ. Closing this letter, we again read the words: *"He that hath an ear, let him hear what the Spirit saith unto the churches."* **Church, the door for revival is still open; Jesus opened it, and no man can close it. Let us pray as never before for one more great revival.** Let us pray for our loved ones who are backslid and our loved ones who have never known the saving grace and the love of Jesus. Let us pray for their salvation as never before, for Jesus is coming. Pray for revival, and again I say, pray for revival.

Unto the Church of Laodicea

Revelation 3:14-22

¹⁴ And unto the angel of the church of the Laodiceans write; These things saith the Amen, the faithful and true witness, the beginning of the creation of God;
¹⁵ I know thy works, that thou art neither cold nor hot: I would thou wert cold or hot.
¹⁶ So then because thou art lukewarm, and neither cold nor hot, I will spue thee out of my mouth.
¹⁷ Because thou sayest, I am rich, and increased with goods, and have need of nothing; and knowest not that thou art wretched, and miserable, and poor, and blind, and naked:
¹⁸ I counsel thee to buy of me gold tried in the fire, that thou mayest be rich; and white raiment, that thou mayest be clothed, and that the shame of thy nakedness do not

appear; and anoint thine eyes with eyesalve, that thou mayest see.

[19] As many as I love, I rebuke and chasten: be zealous therefore, and repent.

[20] Behold, I stand at the door, and knock: if any man hear my voice, and open the door, I will come in to him, and will sup with him, and he with me.

[21] To him that overcometh will I grant to sit with me in my throne, even as I also overcame, and am set down with my Father in his throne.

[22] He that hath an ear, let him hear what the Spirit saith unto the churches.

"*And unto the Angel of the church of the Laodiceans write.*" Laodicea is the last of the seven church ages. **They have a form of Godliness but deny the power of God.** [2 Timothy 3:1-5 – *[1] This know also, that in the last days perilous times shall come. [2] For men shall be lovers of their own selves, covetous, boasters, proud, blasphemers, disobedient to parents, unthankful, unholy, [3] Without natural affection, trucebreakers, false accusers, incontinent, fierce, despisers of those that are good, [4] Traitors, heady, high minded, lovers of pleasures more than lovers of God; [5] Having a form of godliness, but denying the power thereof: from such turn away.*] This letter describes the present-day church world except for the few Philadelphia churches that are still preaching the gospel of Jesus Christ and seeking lost souls for the Master. Is it any wonder why we don't see souls saved, miracles happen and sickness healed? **We should be seeing the Holy Ghost coming down in our services, taking over the service and having His way in the hearts and lives of people as they yield to His presence.** Even in the Pentecostal ranks, we see the spirit of modernism taking its toll. **Churches no longer sing about the blood, no longer preach the full gospel, and the altars are taken out of the churches.** The altars, the meeting places with God, are no longer needed in these churches, because the last thing they want is to meet with God. In the 2012 Democratic Convention, God and any mention of God was taken out of the political platform. Then, because of fear that it might cost them too many votes, it was ramrodded back into their platform. This type of spirit is running wild in the world, and even in the churches. How? **If you deny the truth of God's Word, then you deny God. To deny the miracles of God and the healing power of God, you deny God.**

"These things saith the Amen, the faithful and true witness, the beginning of the creation of God." As we look at Jesus describing himself, He starts with that Amen. As we pray, when we finish, the closing word is Amen. It means the final end, that there is no more. In this seventh letter, Jesus lets us know this is the end. What the church makes of Christ's Amen is up to them. Just like now, our lives are what we make of them. **Where we spend eternity depends on us, not someone else.** Jesus also says that He is the *"beginning of the creation of God."* He was there when the world was formed; He was there when man was made. It was there that God and Jesus first loved their creation, and it's a love that's eternal.

"I know thy works, that thou art neither cold nor hot: I would thou wert cold or hot. So then because thou art lukewarm, and neither cold nor hot, I will spue thee out of my mouth." **Jesus is warning the church of the danger of compromise and the danger of modernism.** When we fail to hold the truth precious, and we reach the place where we are willing to settle for second best, we begin to back away from God. In scripture, when the dis-

ciples found some preaching in Jesus' name, they rebuked them and told them not to preach anymore. Jesus said the disciples were wrong, that if these preachers weren't against Jesus, then they were for Him. **As part of the church of the living God, if we preach any other gospel than the gospel of Jesus Christ, then we are wrong.** I have written about those who have a form of Godliness but deny the power thereof, and from such to turn away. The word also speaks of the blind leaders of the blind. [Matthew 15:12-14 – *12 Then came his disciples, and said unto him, Knowest thou that the Pharisees were offended, after they heard this saying? 13 But he answered and said, Every plant, which my heavenly Father hath not planted, shall be rooted up. 14 Let them alone: they be blind leaders of the blind. And if the blind lead the blind, both shall fall into the ditch.*] and [Luke 6:39 – *And he spake a parable unto them, Can the blind lead the blind? shall they not both fall into the ditch?*] God expects us to err on the side of caution. **We are not to accept anything and everything that claims to be of God, without first checking with God.**

The Word tells us to try the spirits to see if they be of the Lord. [1 John 4:1 – *Beloved, believe not every spirit, but try the spirits whether they are of God: because many false prophets are gone out into the world.*] In the church of Ephesus, the Lord praised the Christians, because before they accepted the profession made by some as being apostles, they were tried and found to be liars. We cannot afford to accept people at face value or by what they say about themselves. **Before I accept all of those who profess to be of God, I want to pray and seek God about the matter.** Our souls are at stake. Do not by any means fall prey to the tricks of the devil. Remember the devil comes in sheep's clothing, and even as an angel of light seeking those whom he may devour. An old saying of the world is "don't believe anything you hear and only half of what you see," and today, we should believe less than half of what we see and none of what we hear. The Laodicean church was a church that accepted anything and everything into their churches; it didn't matter how they believed. This is exactly what's happening in the church world today. **The church is going against God's Word by changing the meaning of the Word to say what the world wants the Word to say, many times saying that people change, so the church must change to meet the needs of the people.** God says that He is the same yesterday, today and forever. The Word doesn't change, and God's Holiness doesn't change; beware, lest you be lead astray.

[Revelation 3:17 – *Because thou sayest, I am rich, and increased with goods, and have need of nothing; and knowest not that thou art wretched, and miserable, and poor, and blind, and naked:*] **Jesus here offers them counsel to buy of Him gold tried in the fire.** He's saying if we want something that's worth something, that's real, that won't pass away, then seek "*Me and the kingdom of heaven,*" the true prize, the true gift that's worth more than life its self. Riches pass away; riches aren't permanent; **when we trust in riches, then we become fools.** [Luke 12:16-21 – *[16] And he spake a parable unto them, saying, The ground of a certain rich man brought forth plentifully: [17] And he thought within himself, saying, What shall I do, because I have no room where to bestow my fruits? [18] And he said, This will I do: I will pull down my barns, and build greater; and there will I bestow all my fruits and my goods. [19] And I will say to my soul, Soul, thou hast much goods laid up for many years; take thine ease, eat, drink, and be merry. [20] But God said unto him, Thou fool, this night thy soul shall be required of thee: then whose shall those things be, which thou hast provided? [21] So is he that layeth up treasure for himself,* *and is not rich toward God*.] When we provide for the natural man and not the spiritual, we think we have everything we want, and in the natural, we may very well have.

But when the natural man dies, the worms devour his body, and so it is for all of us. But the spiritual man lives forever. When God made man, He breathed into him the breath of life, and man became a living soul. [Genesis 2:7 – *And the LORD God formed man of the dust of the ground, and breathed into his nostrils the breath of life; and man became a living soul*.] That soul will never die, and there's only one of two places it can go: either Heaven to be with his maker, or Hell to be with his destroyer. **People need to understand that where we will spend eternity isn't God's decision; it's ours. We live for the Lord, or we live for self. Heaven or Hell, black or white, we make the choice.**

The eye salve that Jesus speaks of is the Holy Ghost that opens our eyes to our condition, so that we can see the true reality of where we stand with God. As Jesus speaks on, He tells us in Revelation 3:19, *"As many as I love, I rebuke and chasten: be zealous therefore, and repent."* **It's not God's will that we should perish but have everlasting life. These seven letters are the warning to the church. Jesus offers the church hope.** [Revelation 3:20-21 – *20 Behold, I stand at the door, and knock: if any man hear my voice, and open the door, I will come in to him, and will sup with him, and he with me. 21 To him that overcometh will I grant to sit with me in my throne, even as I also overcame, and am set down with my Father in his throne*.] *"Behold I stand at the door, and knock; if any man"* means that whosoever will hear and open the door to their heart, Jesus will come into that heart, and he and Jesus will commune or fellowship together; that fellowship means that we will be overcomers and sit with Christ on His throne. What a time that will be to be with Jesus forever and ever. *"He that hath an ear, let him hear what the Spirit saith unto the churches."*

Chapter 3 Review Questions

1. Jesus tells the Sardis church, "I know thy works, that thou hast a name that thou livest and are dead." How can this be?

_____

_____

2. The church at Philadelphia is sometimes called

_____

_____

3. Do you think that we are living in the last days of the Philadelphia church age? _____

4. What does Jesus set before the church?

_____

_____

5. Jesus tells the Philadelphia church He will keep them from what hour? _____

_____

_____

6. What does the word "Amen" mean?

_____

7. Why are we to try the spirits?

_____

_____

8. How is the Laodicean church like the churches of today?

_____

_____

_____

9. What does Jesus mean when He says "Behold I stand at the door and knock?"

_____

_____

_____

Chapter 4

Revelation 4:1-4

¹ After this I looked, and, behold, a door was opened in heaven: and the first voice which I heard was as it were of a trumpet talking with me; which said, Come up hither, and I will shew thee things which must be hereafter.
² And immediately I was in the spirit: and, behold, a throne was set in heaven, and one sat on the throne.
³ And he that sat was to look upon like a jasper and a sardine stone: and there was a rainbow round about the throne, in sight like unto an emerald.
⁴ And round about the throne were four and twenty seats: and upon the seats I saw four and twenty elders sitting, clothed in white raiment; and they had on their heads crowns of gold.

"After this I looked, and, behold, a door was opened in heaven: and the first voice which I heard was as it were of a trumpet talking with me; which said, Come up hither, and I will shew thee things which must be hereafter." To begin this first verse we need to remember what Jesus said in Chapter Three. Jesus told the Philadelphian church that He would open a door for them, and that no man would be able to shut it. This is a promise

to us who believe and trust in the Lord. Our Lord will always make a way for us. Beginning in Chapter Four, Jesus tells us one more time that He has opened a door, a door that gives us access to the throne room of God. After this, John hears the voice of Jesus saying, *"Come up hither."*

Here's where most denominations believe the rapture takes place. And there's some evidence to support the idea. Jesus told the Philadelphian church that He would keep them from the hour of temptation, but what is the hour of temptation? The hour of temptation could very well be just before the mark of the beast comes into effect, or just before people will have to make that final decision to take the mark or become criminals, watching their children starve because they cannot buy or sell without that mark. Surely that would be an hour of decision. No one knows exactly where the rapture is going to take place; we only make assumptions. After chapters 2-3, the church isn't addressed or described anymore. **The common idea is that the church ages end with the rapture of the church. But if we are right and it is the Philadelphian church that's raptured, then the Laodicean church is still left on earth.** Does this become the so-called church of the antichrist, the world church that worships at the feet of the antichrist when he declares himself to be God?

In Verse Two we read, *"And immediately I was in the spirit: and, behold, a throne was set in heaven, and one sat on the throne."* Why does John not try to describe God? Perhaps because **if God were described, man would do his best to make an image of God and worship the image, rather than to worship God**. We can see around us how man has tried to paint pictures of what Jesus Christ looked like. The artists' paintings and what the Bible describes are not the same.

And there were round about the throne, twenty-four seats,

and upon the seats John saw twenty-four elders sitting. These elders were clothed in white raiment, and each one had a crown of gold upon his head. Who are these elders? No one can say for sure. The represented elders could be the twelve apostles of the New Testament and the twelve patriarchs of the Old Testament Israel. **One thing is certain, these elders have already been judged at the judgment seat of Christ and given their reward, as represented by the white robes and crowns of gold that they wear.** Brother Gortner makes this statement: "An interesting fact the reader of Revelation will not fail to note is that the New Jerusalem, the city that lieth foursquare, is represented as having twelve gates, and at the gates twelve angels, and names written there on, which are the names of the twelve tribes of the children of Israel: and the wall of the city as having twelve foundations, and in them the names of the twelve apostles of the Lamb. Rev. 21:12-14."

Revelation 4:5-6

⁵ And out of the throne proceeded lightnings and thunderings and voices: and there were seven lamps of fire burning before the throne, which are the seven Spirits of God. ⁶ And before the throne there was a sea of glass like unto crystal: and in the midst of the throne, and round about the throne, were four beasts full of eyes before and behind.

After seeing the throne and the twenty-four elders, John saw all that was happening; he saw a picture of impending judgment that was coming upon the earth. Out of the throne preceded lightning and thundering and voices. Again, John takes notice: *"and there were seven lamps of fire burning before the throne, which are the seven Spirits of God."* It is believed that these seven spirits are a symbol of the completeness of the Holy Ghost. (We find them in Revelation 1:4. Bible scholars believe them to represent the seven-fold ministry of the Holy Ghost.) **The sea of glass like unto crystal shows us of the transparency of God and the saints in heaven. There's nothing hidden in heaven.** Around about the throne were four beasts full of eyes before and behind, and in verses seven through nine, we will discover more about these four creatures.

Revelation 4:7-9

[7] And the first beast was like a lion, and the second beast like a calf, and the third beast had a face as a man, and the fourth beast was like a flying eagle.
[8] And the four beasts had each of them six wings about him; and they were full of eyes within: and they rest not day and night, saying, Holy, holy, holy, Lord God Almighty, which was, and is, and is to come.
[9] And when those beasts give glory and honour and thanks to him that sat on the throne, who liveth for ever and ever,

To quote Dr. Williams about the four beasts, " 'In the midst' denotes that these living creatures (not beasts) are to be viewed as having vital connection with the judicial authority of God. This special order of created beings so associated with the throne have characteristics representing the entire creation, both man and animal. The four faces signify that they possess the qualities of perfect creatures: the courage and majesty of a lion, patient enduring service of an ox, intelligence of a man, and swiftness in action of an eagle. If we go back to Isaiah [Isaiah 6:1-8 –

¹ In the year that king Uzziah died I saw also the Lord sitting upon a throne, high and lifted up, and his train filled the temple. ² Above it stood the seraphims: each one had six wings; with twain he covered his face, and with twain he covered his feet, and with twain he did fly. ³ And one cried unto another, and said, Holy, holy, holy, is the LORD of hosts: the whole earth is full of his glory. ⁴ And the posts of the door moved at the voice of him that cried, and the house was filled with smoke. ⁵ Then said I, Woe is me! for I am undone; because I am a man of unclean lips, and I dwell in the midst of a people of unclean lips: for mine eyes have seen the King, the LORD of hosts. ⁶ Then flew one of the seraphims unto me, having a live coal in his hand, which he had taken with the tongs from off the altar⁷ And he laid it upon my mouth, and said, Lo, this hath touched thy lips; and thine iniquity is taken away, and thy sin purged. ⁸ Also I heard the voice of the Lord, saying, Whom shall I send, and who will go for us? Then said I, Here am I; send me.] Isaiah describes the Seraphims 'each one had six wings; with twain he covered his face, and with twain he covered his feet and with twain he did fly.' Some say that those beasts are the protectors of the throne. Being full of eyes nothing escapes them. And they cry Holy, Holy, Holy is the Lord God Almighty, they give glory and honor, and thanks to him that sat on the throne who liveth for ever and ever."

Revelation 4:10-11

¹⁰ The four and twenty elders fall down before him that sat on the throne, and worship him that liveth for ever and ever, and cast their crowns before the throne, saying, ¹¹ Thou art worthy, O Lord, to receive glory and honour and power: for thou hast created all things, and for thy pleasure they are and were created.

The twenty-four elders fall down before Him that sat on the throne. There they worship the Lord and give Him glory, honor and praise. They throw or cast their crowns before the Lord to show that nothing is more important than the Lord. He is our Redeemer, our Savior, our High Priest, King of kings, Lord of lords, the Rose of Sharon, the bright and morning star, the Lily of the Valley, Son of David, our deliverer, the Good Shepherd, Immanuel, Prince of Peace, Lamb of God, Light of the world, and Jesus Christ, the Son of God. Worship him; worship him, for He is worthy to be praised.

Chapter 4 Review Questions

1. What did John see in Heaven?

_____

_____

_____

2. Where do most denominations believe the rapture takes place?

_____

_____

3. How many elders are there?

_____

4. Describe the four beasts or creatures.

_____

_____

_____

_____

_____

5. The seven spirits before God are believed to represent the completeness of _____

_____

Chapter 5

Revelation 5:1-4

¹ And I saw in the right hand of him that sat on the throne a book written within and on the backside, sealed with seven seals.
² And I saw a strong angel proclaiming with a loud voice, Who is worthy to open the book, and to loose the seals thereof?
³ And no man in heaven, nor in earth, neither under the earth, was able to open the book, neither to look thereon.
⁴ And I wept much, because no man was found worthy to open and to read the book, neither to look thereon.

This chapter is so important that I will be quoting from several different reference books, the first of which is Dr. Williams' book, *Prevision of History*. "Revelation chapter 5 is a continuation of the vision of Revelation Chapter 4. These chapters contain the key to the rest of the Revelation. In Revelation 4 Christ is worshipped as Creator; in Revelation 5 He is worshipped as Redeemer."

In *Studies of Revelation*, by J. Narver Gartner, he writes: "This fifth chapter occupies a key position in the book, and a correct understanding of it is essential to proper understanding and interpretation of the book as a whole. It is important, therefore, that we get its significance and meaning fixed in our minds, otherwise we shall go astray in our understanding of the chapters which follow."

In *Tyndale's Commentaries,* we read that chapters 4-5 are full of mysteries. "Men feel themselves caught up in the world's evil and its misery, and they cannot break free. Some become rigid determinists, and we must all, at times, feel a sense of hopelessness, and helplessness in the grip of forces stronger than we. This chapter with its seals which no man can break stresses man's inability. But it does not stop there. More important is the fact that through the Lamb the victory is won. The seals are opened and God's purpose is worked out."

Lastly, we want to look at a commentary written by Dr. William Barclay who brings us to Ezekiel 2:9-10. *"And when I looked, behold, an hand was sent unto me; and, lo, a roll of a book was therein; And he spread it before me; and it was written within and without: and there was written therein lamentations, and mourning, and woe."* Barclay tells us, "We must try to visualize the picture which John is drawing. It is taken from the vision of Ezekiel." Ezekiel 2:9 states, *"And when I looked, behold, an hand was sent unto me; and, lo, a roll of a book was therein,"* **The scriptures are similar, but they are given for two different purposes. It's a commission to go to the people of Israel and to preach and warn them to draw near unto God.** *"And he spread it before me; and it was written within and without: and there was written therein lamentations, and mourning, and woe."* Truly, this second verse describes the book in Revelation, as we shall soon see.

The first verse of the fifth chapter speaks of a book written within and on the back, and sealed with seven seals. **Adam's fall**

in the garden took away that divine fellowship man had with God. Adam and Eve were cast out of the garden. The only hope of man being reunited with God in that relationship that Adam and Eve first had with God, is for man to have a Redeemer. **Jesus became our Redeemer, our Savior.** Verse 1 states: *"And I saw a strong angel proclaiming with a loud voice, Who is worthy to open the book, and to loose the seals thereof?"* To show the importance of being worthy to open the book, a strong angel proclaims who is worthy. We know who is worthy; we know who our Redeemer is. In Verse 3 a search is made. *"And no man in heaven, nor in earth, neither under the earth, was able to open the book, neither to look there on."* Pay attention to the words "no man," for truly no man born of woman has the power to alter or change what God will set in motion. Matthew 6:27 says, *"Which of you by taking thought can add one cubit unto his stature."* Jesus was born of a woman, and this is true. The difference is that **Jesus is more than a man. Jesus is God man, more than man; He is the only begotten Son of God.** In Verse 4, John states that *"he wept much because no man was found worthy to open and read the book, neither to look there on."* Visualize, if you will, the distress John must have been under. One can liken it to being burdened to pray, and as we pray we become so overburdened that we just weep, and no words come out, for no words can tell the cry of our heart. I believe this was where John was; there was such a cry, such a desire, and no man could help. Some today see weeping as a sign of weakness, but they are wrong. The shortest verse in the Bible says, *"Jesus wept."* **Weeping isn't a sign of weakness, for even strong men weep. Weeping is a sign of a broken heart, a sign of humbleness.** We need to encourage people to weep before the Lord. I see men tell their little boys, "Don't cry, boys, don't cry; be a man." So, they grow up believing that men should be tough and not cry. Then the Holy Ghost must break down that spirit and teach us to weep and be humble before God. I once, years ago, was listening to a preacher on the radio who made this statement: "When I make an altar call and people come to the front for salvation. I hate to see people come forward weeping and crying because I know they will not stay in the church. They will soon be gone." I remember thinking, "And I know why." They want something that's real, something that they can feel and know that they are walking with God.

Revelation 5:5-6

5 And one of the elders saith unto me, Weep not: behold, the Lion of the tribe of Juda, the Root of David, hath prevailed to open the book, and to loose the seven seals thereof.
6 And I beheld, and, lo, in the midst of the throne and of the four beasts, and in the midst of the elders, stood a Lamb as it had been slain, having seven horns and seven eyes, which are the seven Spirits of God sent forth into all the earth.

"*And one of the elders saith unto me, Weep not: behold the lion of the tribe of Juda.*" The elder here is telling us that **it's Jesus who will open the book; don't weep anymore; the Redeemer has come**. Jesus will break the seals and open the book for us.

"*And I beheld, and, lo, in the midst of the throne, stood a Lamb as it had been slain.*" Dr. Williams writes, "To realize the magnitude and glory of this truth one must understand the Law of Redemption according to Jewish law. Three things could be redeemed; namely, a slave, a wife, and land. To be this Redeemer one must qualify first, by being a near kinsman; second, by having the price to pay; and third, by being willing to pay the price." To illustrate this Law of Redemption, look at the story of Boaz redeeming Elimelech's inheritance and purchasing Ruth to be his wife.

The scripture describes the Lamb as having seven horns and seven eyes which are the seven Spirits of God sent forth into the earth. **The seven spirits of God refer to the Holy Ghost fullness or completeness that was sent forth into the world after Jesus went back to heaven. The horns represent the power of the Holy Ghost – the eyes – the all-seeing power of the Holy Ghost, so that nothing is hid from God.**

Revelation 5:7

[7] And he came and took the book out of the right hand of him that sat upon the throne.

And he came and took the book out of the right hand of God, and **no longer was Satan to have control of the earth**, the earth which groaned for the day of redemption.

Revelation 5:8-10

[8] And when he had taken the book, the four beasts and four and twenty elders fell down before the Lamb, having every one of them harps, and golden vials full of odours, which are the prayers of saints.
[9] And they sung a new song, saying, Thou art worthy to take the book, and to open the seals thereof: for thou wast

slain, and hast redeemed us to God by thy blood out of
every kindred, and tongue, and people, and nation;
¹⁰ And hast made us unto our God kings and priests: and
we shall reign on the earth.

As we read Verse 8, we see a picture of rejoicing in heaven. The Lord is being worshipped and praised. The elders fell down before the Lord, having harps and golden vials full of odors, which are the prayers of the saints. Our prayers aren't wasted. I am sometimes asked, "What good does it do to pray?" **The true prayers of the saints are bottled up, the Word says, in vials full of odors, which are the prayers of the saints.** By this time in scripture, the rapture has taken place and the saints are in heaven with Christ. The Word tells us that *"they sung a new song, saying, thou are worthy,"* because *"thou wast slain and hast redeemed us to God by thy blood out of every kindred, and tongue, and people, and nation."* **What joy there will be in heaven to shout and praise our God, to bow at the feet of Jesus and to know that we've been redeemed.**

In Verse 10, we read that through Jesus we've been made kings and priests unto God, and we shall reign on the earth. Our Lord always keeps his promises.

Revelation 5:11-14

¹¹ And I beheld, and I heard the voice of many angels
round about the throne and the beasts and the elders: and
the number of them was ten thousand times ten thousand,
and thousands of thousands;
¹² Saying with a loud voice, Worthy is the Lamb that was
slain to receive power, and riches, and wisdom, and

strength, and honour, and glory, and blessing.
13 And every creature which is in heaven, and on the earth,
and under the earth, and such as are in the sea, and all
that are in them, heard I saying, Blessing, and honour,
and glory, and power, be unto him that sitteth upon the
throne, and unto the Lamb for ever and ever.
14 And the four beasts said, Amen. And the four and twenty
elders fell down and worshipped him that liveth for ever
and ever.

John said, "I beheld, and I heard the voices of many angels round about the throne, and the number of them was ten thousand times ten thousand and thousands of thousands." I don't know how many that is, but let's just say all the angels, all the saved from the Old Testament, and all the saints saved from the time that Jesus walked the earth. It's kind of mind numbing, but folks it's a "heaping bunch."

Chapter 5 Review Questions

1. Why was no man in heaven, nor in earth able to open the book? _____

_____

_____

2. Why, is Jesus called the root of David?

_____

_____

_____

3. What is kept in the golden vials?

_____

4. What do the seven horns and seven eyes represent?

_____

_____

_____

_____

_____

5. Why are Revelation, chapters 4-5 so very important?

_____

_____

_____

6. What three things must a person fulfill to be a Redeemer?

_____

_____

_____

7. Why can we say that the prayers of the saints are never wasted?

_____

_____

_____

Chapter 6

All the ages and all of the kingdom of heaven have been waiting for the time when Satan, that old deceiver the devil, will be put in his proper place. The breaking of the seventh seal will dictate how this is going to be done. It is the Lord's will to show this, to His faithful servant, John. John then wrote it in a book **so that we who believe will be lifted up in the Lord, knowing that that old dragon will be defeated.**

Revelation 6:1-2

¹ And I saw when the Lamb opened one of the seals, and I heard, as it were the noise of thunder, one of the four beasts saying, Come and see.
² And I saw, and behold a white horse: and he that sat on him had a bow; and a crown was given unto him: and he went forth conquering, and to conquer.

John, in Verse One, tells us that he saw the Lamb open one of the seals, and there was a noise as of thunder. And one of the four beasts (in the Greek it says "living creatures") said to John, *"Come and see."* What John saw was a white horse, and he that sat on him had a bow, and he was given a crown, and he went forth conquering and to conquer. Some fundamentalists believe that the horseman is Christ because he's riding a white horse. **But this horseman is not the same horseman of Revelation 19:11-16.** The horseman in the nineteenth chapter is definitely Christ, as He is named as the Word, the King of kings, while the horseman in Revelation 6:2 isn't named, and this indicates that he's only an imitation. He's the antichrist. He's given a bow, but no arrows, as he rides forth conquering and to conquer. It's believed that he does this without bloodshed, promising peace to the whole earth. The scripture doesn't say that he'll conquer the whole world, but that he goes *"forth conquering, and to conquer."* **The antichrist is only an imitation of Christ, for the antichrist of the coming future will first appear as a well-meaning wise ruler, promising peace and safety, because the world will be entering into turmoil and upheaval.** And he, as the all-wise leader, will one by one bring most, if not all, of the world under his control. But his rule will bring judgment upon the world. He'll get to the place, as we'll later see, that he'll proclaim himself to be God.

Revelation 6:3-4

³ And when he had opened the second seal, I heard the second beast say, Come and see.
⁴ And there went out another horse that was red: and power was given to him that sat thereon to take peace from the earth, and that they should kill one another: and there was given unto him a great sword.

Jesus opened the second seal, the second beast asked John to come and see, and another horseman went forth. This time the horse was red, and he that sat thereon was given power to take peace from the earth that they, the people of the earth, should kill one another. There was given unto him a great sword. **When we talk about taking peace from the earth, we're talking about wars, about mutual slaughter and ethnic cleansing, where one group hates the other and rises up to wipe them off the face of the earth, and about internal violence on the streets (riots).** We've seen some of this already take place, but it's nothing compared to what's coming.

Revelation 6:5-6

⁵ And when he had opened the third seal, I heard the third beast say, Come and see. And I beheld, and lo a black horse; and he that sat on him had a pair of balances in his hand
⁶ And I heard a voice in the midst of the four beasts say, A measure of wheat for a penny, and three measures of barley for a penny; and see thou hurt not the oil and the wine.

And when He had opened the third seal, the third beast (living creature) bid me come and see. What John saw was a black horse, and he that sat upon it had a pair of balances in his hand. And I heard a voice say *"a measure of wheat for a penny, and three measures of barley for a penny, and see thou hurt not the oil and the wine."* **It's believed by commentators that scarcity and famine are the indicated interpretation as to what the black horse and the balances represent.** The second horse brought wars and great calamity to the earth; as we have seen in the past, wars bring shortages of all different kinds. The main theme here is that there will be great shortages of food. The measure of wheat which is about a quart and a half will cost a day's pay. Three measures of barley for a penny or a day's pay.

Think of it this way: **A loaf of bread will cost a whole day's wages**. There are two trains of thought on the last part of Verse 6, where the horseman is told not to damage the oil and the wine. Weymouth's commentary supposes this to mean that these luxuries are still to be enjoyed by the rich. **The other reasonable interpretation could mean the medical values afforded by the olive oil and the wine was to be spared by a still-loving God even as He brings judgment upon a Godless world.**

Revelation 6:7-8

> [7] *And when he had opened the fourth seal, I heard the voice of the fourth beast say, Come and see.*
> [8] *And I looked, and behold a pale horse: and his name that sat on him was Death, and Hell followed with him. And power was given unto them over the fourth part of the earth, to kill with sword, and with hunger, and with death, and with the beasts of the earth.*

And when Jesus had opened the fourth seal, the fourth beast said to come and see. John states, *"And I looked and behold a pale horse: and his name that sat on him was Death, and Hell followed with him. And the power was given unto them over a fourth part of the earth, to kill with sword, and with hunger and with death, and with the beasts that inhabit the earth."* With the second horseman bringing wars and death, and the third horseman bringing famine and starvation and death, now **the fourth horseman is given power to destroy the lives of one-fourth of the population**. What a terrible time it will be on the face of the earth.

Can you visualize how many are going to die? The world

population as of May 2017 is over seven billion (7,000,000,000). **One-fourth of that comes to one billion, seven hundred fifty million (1,750,000,000), give or take, that will be destroyed by death.** I say "give or take" because we have no idea how many will be killed by the second and third horseman.

Revelation 6:9-11

⁹ And when he had opened the fifth seal, I saw under the altar the souls of them that were slain for the word of God, and for the testimony which they held:
¹⁰ And they cried with a loud voice, saying, How long, O Lord, holy and true, dost thou not judge and avenge our blood on them that dwell on the earth?
¹¹ And white robes were given unto every one of them; and it was said unto them, that they should rest yet for a little season, until their fellowservants also and their brethren, that should be killed as they were, should be fulfilled.

And He opened the fifth seal, and John saw under the altar the souls of them that were slain for the Word of God and for the testimony which they held. Who are these souls? **These are the souls of those who die for Christ after the rapture of the church.** They refuse to take the "mark of the beast" and are killed as punishment. The Word states that they cried with a loud voice asking Christ how long was He going to wait to *"judge and avenge their blood on them that dwell on the earth?"* Verse 11 tells us that white robes were given unto every one of them. White robes represent the Holiness and Righteousness of God. These souls were told that they should rest yet for a little season, until their fellow servants and their brethren that should be killed as they were, should be fulfilled.

As we look at this group of souls we might ask, who are they? I personally believe that **they are backsliders who missed the rapture. They are also those who have knowledge of the scriptures and know that to die for Christ is their only hope of salvation.** I don't believe, as some do, that there will be a great revival after the rapture of the church. I can see no basis for this belief. As we have seen, the Holy Ghost is no longer on earth; He is before the throne of glory. Those who miss the rapture must live on courage and grit, knowing this is their only hope. **Know what you believe, and unless scripture corrects you and shows that you are wrong, believe what you know and live what you believe.**

Revelation 6:12-17

[12] And I beheld when he had opened the sixth seal, and, lo, there was a great earthquake; and the sun became black as sackcloth of hair, and the moon became as blood;
[13] And the stars of heaven fell unto the earth, even as a fig tree casteth her untimely figs, when she is shaken of a mighty wind.
[14] And the heaven departed as a scroll when it is rolled together; and every mountain and island were moved out of their places.
[15] And the kings of the earth, and the great men, and the rich men, and the chief captains, and the mighty men, and every bondman, and every free man, hid themselves in the dens and in the rocks of the mountains;
[16] And said to the mountains and rocks, Fall on us, and hide us from the face of him that sitteth on the throne, and

from the wrath of the Lamb:
[17] For the great day of his wrath is come; and who shall be able to stand?

After Christ opens the sixth seal, John describes a great earthquake; the sun became as black as sackcloth of hair, and the moon became as blood. Dr. William Barclay tells us that "John is using pictures very familiar to his Jewish readers. The Jews always regarded the end as a time when the earth would be shattered and there would be cosmic upheaval and destruction." **The earthquake is the symbol of God shaking the earth, and man still won't listen or take heed.**

In Verse 13, we read, *"and the stars of heaven fell unto the earth."* Some writers claim that all these events are a forewarning of a time when all governments will fail and go under. It will be a time spiritually of great despair. [Hebrews 12:25-28 – *[25] See that ye refuse not him that speaketh. For if they escaped not who refused him that spake on earth, much more shall not we escape, if we turn away from him that speaketh from heaven: [26] Whose voice then shook the earth: but now he hath promised, saying, Yet once more I shake not the earth only, but also heaven. [27] And this word, Yet once more, signifieth the removing of those things that are shaken, as of things that are made, that those things which cannot be shaken may remain. [28] Wherefore we receiving a kingdom which cannot be moved, let us have grace, whereby we may serve God acceptably with reverence and godly fear:*] **Where prophesy is concerned, scripture must interpret scripture.** Over and over the Word speaks of God shaking the earth, and the heavens will also be shaken. **Spiritual wickedness will also be shaken as men and women try to hide themselves from the face of Almighty God.**

In Verse 15, John talks about the kings of the earth; and great men; and rich men, military men, bond men, and free men hiding in dens or caves and in the rock of the mountains. In Verse 16, they call to the mountains and rocks to fall upon them and *"hide us from the face of Him that sitteth on the throne, and from the wrath of the Lamb."*

Verse 17 says, *"For the great day of His wrath is come and who shall be able to stand?"* The old order that the world has known will be swept away, according to John Phillips' commentary on Revelations. "Even the wicked men will have to acknowledge the sovereignty of God." Dr. Elizabeth Williams in *Prevision of History* states of the wicked, "In their fear, they acknowledge their inability to escape or to stand, yet they do not repent but harden their hearts. The judgment scenes to appear later show their blasphemy of God (Revelation 16:9-11 (KJV) [9] *And men were scorched with great heat, and blasphemed the name of God, which hath power over these plagues: and they repented not to give him glory.* [10] *And the fifth angel poured out his vial upon the seat of the beast; and his kingdom was full of darkness; and they gnawed their tongues for pain,* [11] *And blasphemed the God of heaven because of their pains and their sores, and repented not of their deeds.*) and contempt for Christ. (Revelation 19:19 (KJV) *And I saw the beast, and the kings of the earth, and their armies, gathered together to make war against him that sat on the horse, and against his army.*)" It would seem to me that it would be far better to repent and seek God for forgiveness. **Instead, they have so hardened their hearts, that no matter the outcome, they will not admit their folly before God. They consider hell is better than repentance, may God have mercy upon their souls.**

My Christian brothers and sisters, what lies ahead for the world is terrible, but it is coming. As we look at the world around us, we can already see the beginnings of these things. We hear of earthquakes around the world. Volcanoes erupt and cloud the sun in parts of the world. There are riots in the streets because people do not get their way, and in these conditions, lawlessness is rampant. People feel that if you have something that they want, they have the right to take it. Let us pray that Jesus returns very soon. The Lord is the only hope for the believers in Him. Let us go ahead and see what else God has in store for this poor world.

Chapter 6 Review Questions

1. Who is the rider of the white horse?

_____

2. What power is given to the rider of the red horse?

_____

_____

3. The black horse rider carries a pair of balances; what is

this believed to mean? _____

_____

_____

4. The pale horse rider is named and what follows him is

named. What is his name and what follows him?

_____

_____

5. What do the white robes represent?

_____

_____

6. Where will men go to hide from God?

_____

_____

7. What does the fifth angel do?

_____

_____

8. What are the results of what the fifth angel did?

_____

_____

Chapter 7

What we see as we begin to look at this seventh chapter is that we are looking at a parenthesis. In other words, what we have here are events that do not happen in chronological order. **The events described in this chapter do not take place or happen till later in the upcoming chapters of this book when the beast comes to power and conquers all that would stand in his way.** When the seals are broken and all that holds the devil back is removed, it can only be a matter of time till everything will come to a head. As we study Revelation, we can be assured that our God wants all the church to know what lies ahead for those who will miss the rapture.

Revelation 7:1-3

[1] And after these things I saw four angels standing on the four corners of the earth, holding the four winds of the earth, that the wind should not blow on the earth, nor on the sea, nor on any tree.
[2] And I saw another angel ascending from the east, having the seal of the living God: and he cried with a loud voice to the four angels, to whom it was given to hurt the earth and the sea, [3] Saying, Hurt not the earth, neither the sea, nor the trees, till we have sealed the servants of our God in their foreheads.

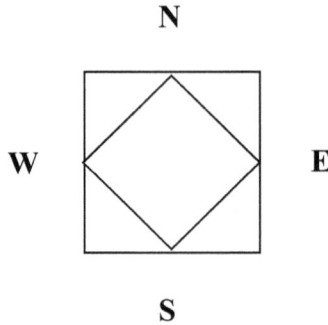

The first thing John tells us as we look at the first verse is *"I saw four angels standing on the four corners of the earth, holding the four winds of the earth."* Stopping here, you might say the earth is round; it doesn't have four corners. But, if we look at what was believed **in John's day, it was held to be true that the world was flat. This was the popular belief even as recent as the 1400's.** If you took off sailing, after going so far, you would simply fall off the edge of the world. If we look at the earth and find north, east, south and west, it could appear that the earth was flat. These four angels were holding the winds or keeping the winds from blowing on the earth. In Verse 2, John saw another angel ascending from the east, having the seal of the living God, and he cried with a loud voice to the four angels to whom it was given to hurt the earth and the sea. Verse 3 says, *"Hurt not the earth, neither the sea, nor the trees, till we have sealed the servants of our God in their foreheads."* **Some have tried to identify these as the raptured church. But this cannot be so; the rapture has already taken place.** The saints have sung the song of the redeemed; they have witnessed the Lamb breaking six of the seven seals that bind the Book. In Verse 4, it states: *"And I heard the number of them which were sealed."*

Revelation 7:4-8

⁴ And I heard the number of them which were sealed: and there were sealed an hundred and forty and four thousand of all the tribes of the children of Israel.
⁵ Of the tribe of Juda were sealed twelve thousand. Of the tribe of Reuben were sealed twelve thousand. Of the tribe of Gad were sealed twelve thousand.
⁶ Of the tribe of Aser were sealed twelve thousand. Of the tribe of Nepthalim were sealed twelve thousand. Of the tribe of Manasses were sealed twelve thousand.
⁷ Of the tribe of Simeon were sealed twelve thousand. Of the tribe of Levi were sealed twelve thousand. Of the tribe of Issachar were sealed twelve thousand.
⁸ Of the tribe of Zabulon were sealed twelve thousand. Of the tribe of Joseph were sealed twelve thousand. Of the tribe of Benjamin were sealed twelve thousand.

John heard how many were to be sealed, 144,000 of all the tribes of the children of Israel. **There's no mistaking who these 144,000 are. They are Jews and not Gentiles.** There are twelve thousand sealed out of each tribe of the twelve tribes of Israel. In *Prevision of History, A Study of Daniel and Revelation*, Dr. Williams notes that "Dan and Ephriam are not named among the twelve tribes, but Joseph and Levi are named. The name of Joseph probably is substituted for Ephraim since Ephraim and Manasseh were sons of Joseph, and Manasseh's tribe is named in this passage. Levi, the priestly tribe, is named with its twelve thousand sealed. Why Dan is omitted is not made known. Scott, as well as other expositors expressed the possibility of Dan being omitted, since this tribe was the first to go into idolatry." **We will again** see the 144,000 standing with the Lamb on Mount Zion in Chapter 14.

Revelation 7:9-17

⁹ After this I beheld, and, lo, a great multitude, which no man could number, of all nations, and kindreds, and people, and tongues, stood before the throne, and before the Lamb, clothed with white robes, and palms in their hands;
¹⁰ And cried with a loud voice, saying, Salvation to our God which sitteth upon the throne, and unto the Lamb.
¹¹ And all the angels stood round about the throne, and about the elders and the four beasts, and fell before the throne on their faces, and worshipped God,
¹² Saying, Amen: Blessing, and glory, and wisdom, and thanksgiving, and honour, and power, and might, be unto our God for ever and ever. Amen.
¹³ And one of the elders answered, saying unto me, What are these which are arrayed in white robes? and whence came they?
¹⁴ And I said unto him, Sir, thou knowest. And he said to me, These are they which came out of great tribulation, and have washed their robes, and made them white in the blood of the Lamb.
¹⁵ Therefore are they before the throne of God, and serve him day and night in his temple: and he that sitteth on the throne shall dwell among them.
¹⁶ They shall hunger no more, neither thirst any more; neither shall the sun light on them, nor any heat.
¹⁷ For the Lamb which is in the midst of the throne shall feed them, and shall lead them unto living fountains of wa-

ters: and God shall wipe away all tears from their eyes.

Here we are looking at another parenthesis. I, through much prayer, believe that these are the raptured saints, (the church of Jesus Christ) that He has taken to heaven to be with Him. We need to be aware that the events in this chapter are not in chronological order. To believe that they are is a grave mistake in interpretation. The scripture in Verse 9 speaks of John *"seeing a great multitude which no man could number of all nations, and kindreds, and people, and tongues,"* standing before the Lamb clothed with white robes, and palms in their hands.

As I read the scriptures and God begins to open the Word to me, He is showing me something different than most Bible scholars believe. First, I do not believe that the church is raptured before any of the tribulation begins. Second, I believe that when the church is raptured that the Holy Ghost leaves this world with the raptured church. The Holy Ghost was sent to the church to be our comforter and companion to lead us into a closer walk with God. The Holy Ghost was sent to the saints (the church), and when the saints are caught away, the Holy Ghost leaves with the saints, his job here having been completed.

We have already seen the Holy Ghost before the throne of God. In Chapter Five, we see the seven spirits of God before the throne. These spirits represent the Holy Ghost; the saints are also there because they have sung the "new song," white robes have been given unto them and they have been told to rest and wait.

There is a teaching that is being taught in denominational churches today that I am strongly opposed to. This teaching can and will cause many to miss heaven if people are persuaded to believe it. This teaching is that after the rapture of the church, there will be a great worldwide revival. In this revival, there are supposed to be great multitudes of people that will be saved. I can find no basis for this belief. I truly hope that those who are teaching this are right, but I do not believe it to be so. For this to be right, the Holy Ghost that was sent to be our comforter will have to remain here after the saints are caught away. I personally do not believe this to be so, however, if you do, that is between you and God.

The down side to this belief is that people will say that if they miss the rapture, they will get saved during the great revival period after the rapture. The last thing that people need is a false sense of security, a false hope that isn't there. I know there will be some saved in the tribulation. They will give their lives for Christ and by the word of their testimony. However, there will be no great multitudes that no man could number. Again, I sincerely hope that I am wrong, but I cannot see it.

The Word in Verse 10 speaks of the saints crying *"Salvation to our God . . . and unto the Lamb."* Such praises there will be! Verse 13 states: *"one of the elders answered, saying unto me, What are these which are arrayed in white robes? and whence came they? And I said unto him, Sir, thou knowest."* Then the elder answers John's question in Verse 14: *"These are they which came out of great tribulation, and have washed their robes, and made them white in the blood of the Lamb."*

These next verses (9-17) show that the church will go into the beginning of the "great" tribulation. The church won't go in very far because of what's going to be taking place, but it will go into the beginning of it. In the letter to the Philadelphian church, Jesus said in Revelation 3:12, *"Him that overcometh will I make a pillar in the temple of my God, and he shall go no more out, and I will write upon him the name of my God . . . and I will write upon him my new name."* Revelation 7:15 goes on to tell us,

"Therefore are they before the throne of God, and serve him day and night in his temple: and He that sitteth on the throne shall dwell among them." I don't know if you catch the sameness of these two scriptures, but to me God says they are the same.

The time of great sorrows is when the four horsemen are given power over the earth, also over one fourth of the men, women and children, who will be killed. What great sorrow there will be as people bury their dead loved ones. Will the church be here as all of this takes place? I would like to say no, but I cannot. Somewhere in the first three-and-one-half years the church will be raptured, but just where, I cannot say. I hope in the very beginning, but we are not given that information. I know that there are some who are trying to pinpoint the time as here or there, but rest assured that no one knows but God. Therefore, we must stay ready to meet Jesus at any time.

Verse 17 states that **we shall be lead unto living fountains of waters, and God shall wipe away all tears from our eyes.** Praise be to the Lamb of God, and like the song says:

> *Won't it be wonderful there,*
> *Having no burdens to bear,*
> *Joyfully singing with heart bells all ringing,*
> *Won't it be wonderful there.*

Chapter 7 Review Questions

1. Chapter 7 is a parenthesis. What is a parenthesis?

_____

_____

2. The four angels that held the winds were told not to hurt the earth until what could be done?

_____

_____

3. How many souls were sealed?

_____

4. How many from each tribe?

_____

5. Who makes up the great multitude standing before the Lamb? _____

_____

6. Will the church go into the tribulation period? _____

7. Will there be a great revival after the rapture? _____

8. What makes you believe your answer to Questions 6 and 7?

_____

Chapter 8

Revelation 8:1-2

¹ And when he had opened the seventh seal, there was silence in heaven about the space of half an hour.
² And I saw the seven angels which stood before God; and to them were given seven trumpets.

"*And when he had opened the seventh seal, there was silence in heaven about the space of half an hour.*" What's this silence for? There are two thoughts on this: Irwin's *Bible Commentary* points out "that this silence corresponds with the customary interval in the worship of the Jewish sanctuary, during which the priests went in to offer incense while worshippers waited in the outer court in silence." **I believe that the impending silence in heaven is to prepare heaven for the judgment which is to follow.**

As we look at the Revelation period, we see that it is seven years long and is divided into two parts. Each part consists of three-and-one-half years. The first three-and-a-half years are the time of great sorrows. The last three-and-a-half years are when the great wrath of God is poured out upon the earth. It's hard for one to think that man's heart will be so hardened, that instead of crying out for forgiveness from God,

he will curse God for his troubles.

The judgments are going to be so great and terrible, the like of which the earth has never seen before. This silence is God preparing Himself for what He is going to unleash on the earth and mankind. For thousands of years God has tried to get man's attention, even sending His only begotten Son, and still men won't turn from their wicked ways. And in all this time, God still loved His creation. Now the end has finally come; judgment must be poured out; and God still loves man. As angry as God was when He destroyed the earth by water, still one man found favor in the eyes of the Lord. One man can and does make a difference with God.

John said, "*I saw the seven angels which stood before God and to them were given seven trumpets.*" Who are these seven angels? In Tyndale's commentary, he states that Tobit 12:15 (a book in the Apocrypha) says, "I am Raphael, one of the seven holy angels which present the prayers of the saints, and which go in and out before the glory of the Holy One." Also, in the book of Enoch (an Apocryphal book that is quoted in the New Testament), Chapter 20 lists these six angels: Uriel, Raphael, Raguel, Michael, Saraqael and Gabriel. Tyndale adds one to that for a total of seven: Uriel, Raphael, Raguel, Michael, Saraqael, Gabriel and Remiel, who are in a position of authority. We know that Michael and Gabriel are Archangels and believe that the other five are also Archangels. This may or may not be the case; it really doesn't matter what their names are. **These seven angels are each given a trumpet to herald judgment as it comes on man.**

Revelation 8:3-5

[3] *And another angel came and stood at the altar, having a*

golden censer; and there was given unto him much
incense, that he should offer it with the prayers of all
saints upon the golden altar which was before the throne.
⁴ And the smoke of the incense, which came with the
prayers of the saints, ascended up before God out of the
angel's hand.
⁵ And the angel took the censer, and filled it with fire of the
altar, and cast it into the earth: and there were voices, and
thunderings, and lightnings, and an earthquake.

Another angel appears and stands at the altar having a golden censer; and he was given much incense to offer up with the prayers of all the saints upon the golden altar that is before the great throne of God. The smoke of the incense, which came with the prayers of the saints, went up before God. And the angel took the censer, filled it with fire from the altar and cast it into the earth, and there were voices and thundering and lightening and an earthquake. **All of these things (these terrible judgments) will be poured out on the earth as a result of all the prayers of the saints.** As the angels sound the trumpets one by one, deliberate judgments will be poured out upon the world. **Saints, all your prayers are not wasted. They are precious in the sight of the Lord,** as we see here in Revelation, Chapter 8. Keep praying and keep holding to your faith; God will move in our behalf, because this is a promise from God.

Revelation 8:6-7

⁶ And the seven angels which had the seven trumpets
prepared themselves to sound.
⁷ The first angel sounded, and there followed hail and fire

mingled with blood, and they were cast upon the earth:
and the third part of trees was burnt up, and all green
grass was burnt up.

The trumpets have been given out; the angels are preparing to sound the trumpets; as each trumpet sounds, judgment will be poured out on the inhabitants of the earth. Scripture states that one third of all the trees were burnt up and all green grass was burnt up. **Modern man would call it global warming, the sun getting too hot. No matter how man tries to seek an answer, be sure they won't look to God.** This trumpet is very self-explanatory; this is going to happen, and nothing can change it; judgment has come upon the land.

Revelation 8:8-9

[8] And the second angel sounded, and as it were a great
mountain burning with fire was cast into the sea: and the
third part of the sea became blood;
[9] And the third part of the creatures which were in the sea,
and had life, died; and the third part of the ships were
destroyed.

And the second angel sounded his trumpet, and as it were a great mountain burning with fire was cast into the sea. **Note, John didn't say that it was a mountain that was on fire and cast into the sea, but *like* a great mountain.** Dr. Williams believes: "A great mountain-like volcano erupts in the sea and one-third part of the sea becomes blood. This affects the sea's food supply. Also one-third of the ocean's ships of transportation are destroyed." John Phillips' commentary *Exploring Revelation* also agrees with Dr. Williams. J. Narver Gortner in *Studies in Revelation* believes: "Here it is not recorded that a great mountain, but as it were a great mountain burning with fire was cast into the sea. It would seem that what is meant is that a great meteoric mass from some distant planet or sun . . . will approach the atmosphere of the earth, and penetrate it, and fall into the sea directed in its course by the hand of God."

The Word further says a third part of the sea became blood, resulting in one-third of the creatures that live in the sea dying, and one third of the ships being destroyed. Is it going to be a volcano or a meteor? That you must decide for yourself. **I personally believe that it will be a meteor, because the Word says it was cast into the sea; to me a volcano that erupts in the sea is not the same as being cast into the sea. But however it happens; it's still going to happen.**

Revelation 8:10-11

> [10] *And the third angel sounded, and there fell a great star from heaven, burning as it were a lamp, and it fell upon the third part of the rivers, and upon the fountains of waters;*
> [11] *And the name of the star is called Wormwood: and the third part of the waters became wormwood; and many men died of the waters, because they were made bitter.*

The tenth and eleventh verses are just what they say they are; the third angel sounds the trumpet, and there falls a great star from heaven, burning as it were a lamp. **This star can easily be described as a meteor that falls to the earth.** We have meteors that fall every day. Most burn up in the atmosphere (some very small ones do hit the earth). **This star or meteor has a name, Wormwood. It isn't small and does a lot of damage. It fell upon the third part of the rivers and upon the fountains of water; the third part of the waters became wormwood; and many men died of the waters because they were made bitter.** In *Studies in Revelation*, Rev. Gortner wrote about an article that was in the *Pentecostal Evangel* (August 9, 1947), and in it appeared the following paragraph: "Scientists are weighing the possibility of exploding an atomic bomb in the midst of storm clouds to create a literal rain of death. The bombing plane would fly high above the storm clouds, and would locate the target by radar. The explosion of the atomic bomb would cause the clouds to be emptied and the rain would be poisoned with the deadly by product of the bomb's explosion. Does it not remind you of Revelation 8:11?" **Man continually tries to find more and more ways to kill his fellow man. The scripture tells us that many men died from drinking the water because it was made bitter, or in other words, that it was poisoned.**

Revelation 8:12-13

[12] And the fourth angel sounded, and the third part of the sun was smitten, and the third part of the moon, and the third part of the stars; so as the third part of them was darkened, and the day shone not for a third part of it, and the night likewise.
[13] And I beheld, and heard an angel flying through the midst of heaven, saying with a loud voice, Woe, woe, woe, to the inhabiters of the earth by reason of the other voices

of the trumpet of the three angels, which are yet to sound!

The fourth angel sounds the trumpets and terrible things happen: *". . . the third part of the sun was smitten, and a third part of the moon and the third part of the stars, so as the third part of them was darkened."* **According to John, the sun didn't shine for a third part of the day, and the moon likewise didn't shine for a third part of the night. In the Word, the Lord speaks of there being signs and wonders in the heavens, in the sun and moon and the stars.** Read some of the accounts:

Isaiah 5:30

> *And in that day they shall roar against them like the roaring of the sea: and if one look unto the land, behold darkness and sorrow, and the light is darkened in the heavens thereof.*

Amos 8:9

> *And it shall come to pass in that day, saith the Lord GOD, that I will cause the sun to go down at noon, and I will darken the earth in the clear day:*

Jeremiah 4:23, 28

> *[23] I beheld the earth, and, lo, it was without form, and void; and the heavens, and they had no light.*
> *[28] For this shall the earth mourn, and the heavens above be black: because I have spoken it, I have purposed it, and will not repent, neither will I turn back from it.*

Joel 2:10, 30-31

[10] The earth shall quake before them; the heavens shall tremble: the sun and the moon shall be dark, and the stars shall withdraw their shining:
[30] And I will shew wonders in the heavens and in the earth, blood, and fire, and pillars of smoke.
[31] The sun shall be turned into darkness, and the moon into blood, before the great and the terrible day of the LORD come.

Matthew 24:29

Immediately after the tribulation of those days shall the sun be darkened, and the moon shall not give her light, and the stars shall fall from heaven, and the powers of the heavens shall be shaken:

Mark 13:24-26

[24] But in those days, after that tribulation, the sun shall be darkened, and the moon shall not give her light,
[25] And the stars of heaven shall fall, and the powers that are in heaven shall be shaken.
[26] And then shall they see the Son of man coming in the clouds with great power and glory.

Acts 2:19-21

[19] And I will shew wonders in heaven above, and signs in the earth beneath; blood, and fire, and vapour of smoke:

²⁰ The sun shall be turned into darkness, and the moon into blood, before that great and notable day of the Lord come: ²¹ And it shall come to pass, that whosoever shall call on the name of the Lord shall be saved.

God is letting all this happen for man's sake; it's still not too late. In Verse 13, John states that he *"heard an angel flying through the midst of heaven, saying with a loud voice. Woe, woe, woe to the inhibiters of the earth by reason of the other voices of the trumpet of the three angels which are yet to sound!"* There's controversy about this angel that flies through the midst of heaven. In the King James Version (KJV) it's called an angel, and in other translations the angel is called an eagle. Scholars say the best manuscripts agree that it's an eagle that flies through heaven. **I personally will stay with the King James Version. It's been with us for four hundred years. Why? Because it was ordained of God and has lead hundreds of millions of people to the saving knowledge of Jesus Christ.** The Finis Jennings Dake Bible states that "angels can fly through the heavens even though they do not have wings." I know that with God all things are possible, that the dumb ass spoke to Balaam with a man's voice, so God could cause an eagle to speak. I will go, however, with the vision of John and believe that it was an angel of the Lord. **The angel is sounding out a warning to the earth that there are still three trumpets yet to sound, and each trumpet judgment gets worse and worse.**

Chapter 8 Review Questions

1. There will be silence in heaven for how long?

_____

2. How many angels were given trumpets?

_____

3. What was offered up on the golden altar?

_____

_____

_____

4. What does the Bible say was burned up when the first

trumpet sounded? _____

_____

_____

5. How much of the sea will become blood?

_____

6. What was the name of the star that fell from heaven?

_____

7. What is the warning the angel that flies through the air is sounding out?

_____

_____

_____

_____

Chapter 9

The sounding of the fifth trumpet and the first of the three woes is unleashed upon man. John tells us that he saw a star fall from heaven unto the earth and to him was given the key to the bottomless pit.

Revelation 9:1-12

[1] And the fifth angel sounded, and I saw a star fall from heaven unto the earth: and to him was given the key of the bottomless pit.
[2] And he opened the bottomless pit; and there arose a smoke out of the pit, as the smoke of a great furnace; and the sun and the air were darkened by reason of the smoke of the pit.
[3] And there came out of the smoke locusts upon the earth: and unto them was given power, as the scorpions of the earth have power.
[4] And it was commanded them that they should not hurt the grass of the earth, neither any green thing, neither any tree; but only those men which have not the seal of God in their foreheads.
[5] And to them it was given that they should not kill them, but that they should be tormented five months: and their

torment was as the torment of a scorpion, when he striketh a man.

⁶ And in those days shall men seek death, and shall not find it; and shall desire to die, and death shall flee from them.

⁷ And the shapes of the locusts were like unto horses prepared unto battle; and on their heads were as it were crowns like gold, and their faces were as the faces of men.

⁸ And they had hair as the hair of women, and their teeth were as the teeth of lions.

⁹ And they had breastplates, as it were breastplates of iron; and the sound of their wings was as the sound of chariots of many horses running to battle.

¹⁰ And they had tails like unto scorpions, and there were stings in their tails: and their power was to hurt men five months.

¹¹ And they had a king over them, which is the angel of the bottomless pit, whose name in the Hebrew tongue is Abaddon, but in the Greek tongue hath his name Apollyon.

¹² One woe is past; and, behold, there come two woes more hereafter.

There's some dispute among scholars as to who the star is; some say he's a fallen angel, others Satan, others that he's a trusted angel of the Lord. First, he's given the key to the bottomless pit. When he opens the bottomless pit and smoke rises up out of the pit, the smoke is so great that it darkens the sun. *"And there came out of the smoke locusts upon the earth: and unto them was given power, as the scorpions of the earth have power."* **These locusts are not ordinary locust but spiritual beings.**

The smoke and fire doesn't harm them. They are imprisoned in the bottomless pit and cannot come out until the angel opens the door. They have power to hurt man. It was commanded unto them that they were not to hurt the grass of the earth neither any green thing, not any tree, but only men who were not sealed to God. These locusts weren't to kill mankind but to torment man, and their torment was to last five months. Their torment was to be like the sting of a scorpion when it stings man. For five months this was to go on. **The pain and torment is to be so great that men will seek death and won't be able to find it. They will desire to die, and the Bible says that death will flee from them.** They will hurt so bad they cannot stand the pain; they will try to kill themselves and not be able to die.

We see a description of these locust in the seventh and eighth verses: *"And the shapes of the locusts were like unto horses prepared unto battle; and on their heads were as it were crowns like gold, and their faces were as the faces of men. And they had hair as the hair of women, and their teeth were as the teeth of lions."* These creatures are not a pleasant sight. Verse 10 tells us they had tails like a scorpion, there were stings in their tails, and they had the power to hurt man for five months. **Think of being stung by a scorpion, and then that going on for five months without stopping. No wonder men and women will seek to die, and yet, they won't be able to die.** The Bible states: *"And they had a king over them,"* and this speaks of intelligence, that they aren't just dumb creatures but are commanded by their king, which is the angel of the bottomless pit whose name in Hebrew is A-bad-don and in the Greek A-polely-on. Verse 12 tells us that one woe is past and that there are two more woes still to be poured out on man. **God's judgment is truly fearful.**

Revelation 9:13-21

13 And the sixth angel sounded, and I heard a voice from the four horns of the golden altar which is before God,
14 Saying to the sixth angel which had the trumpet, Loose the four angels which are bound in the great river Euphrates.
15 And the four angels were loosed, which were prepared for an hour, and a day, and a month, and a year, for to slay the third part of men.
16 And the number of the army of the horsemen were two hundred thousand thousand: and I heard the number of them.
17 And thus I saw the horses in the vision, and them that sat on them, having breastplates of fire, and of jacinth, and brimstone: and the heads of the horses were as the heads of lions; and out of their mouths issued fire and smoke and brimstone.
18 By these three was the third part of men killed, by the fire, and by the smoke, and by the brimstone, which issued out of their mouths.
19 For their power is in their mouth, and in their tails: for their tails were like unto serpents, and had heads, and with them they do hurt.
20 And the rest of the men which were not killed by these plagues yet repented not of the works of their hands, that they should not worship devils, and idols of gold, and silver, and brass, and stone, and of wood: which neither can see, nor hear, nor walk:
21 Neither repented they of their murders, nor of their sorceries, nor of their fornication, nor of their thefts.

Verse 13 states: *"And the sixth angel sounded, and I heard a voice from the four horns of the golden altar which is before God,"* As we remember what we've studied so far, **the souls of the saints** (Revelation 6:10 – *And they cried with a loud voice, saying, How long, O Lord, holy and true, dost thou not judge and avenge our blood on them that dwell on the earth?*) **were calling for God to avenge them**. Then in Revelation 8:3-5 (*³ And another angel came and stood at the altar, having a golden censer; and there was given unto him much incense, that he should offer it with the prayers of all saints upon the golden altar which was before the throne. ⁴ And the smoke of the incense, which came with the prayers of the saints, ascended up before God out of the angel's hand. ⁵ And the angel took the censer, and filled it with fire of the altar, and cast it into the earth: and there were voices, and thunderings, and lightnings, and an earthquake.*) that **the prayers of all the saints and much incense were offered upon the golden altar which is before the throne.** Now we hear a voice coming from the four horns of the golden altar. In the Old Testament, God gave instructions on how the altar was to be made: The altar was to have a horn at each corner. In 1 Kings 2:28-30, we read of how Joab fled to the temple, and taking hold of the horns of the altar, prayed to God. (*²⁸ Then tidings came to Joab: for Joab had turned after Adonijah, though he turned not after Absalom. And Joab fled unto the tabernacle of the LORD, and caught hold on the horns of the altar. ²⁹ And it was told king Solomon that Joab was fled unto the tabernacle of the LORD; and, behold, he is by the altar. Then Solomon sent Benaiah the son of Jehoiada, saying, Go, fall upon him. ³⁰ And Benaiah came to the tabernacle of the LORD, and said unto him, Thus saith the king, Come forth. And he said, Nay; but I will die here. And Benaiah brought the king word again, saying, Thus said Joab, and thus he answered me.*)

We hear preachers, myself included, preaching that we need to get ahold of the horns of the altar. What we mean is to get in contact with God to pray and make our partitions known to God. Here in Verse 13, **these prayers that are on the golden altar cry out for justice, to be avenged of God on this evil world.**

The voice speaks, in Verse 14, to the sixth angel and tells the angel to turn loose the four angels which are bound in the river Euphrates (Eu-phra'tes). These angels are evil, and they were bound to protect mankind. We read in the scripture of angels being bound in the books of Peter and Jude. (*2 Peter 2:4 – For if God spared not the angels that sinned, but cast them down to hell, and delivered them into chains of darkness, to be reserved unto judgment;* **and** *Jude 1:6 – And the angels which kept not their first estate, but left their own habitation, he hath reserved in everlasting chains under darkness unto the judgment of the great day.)* God is no respecter of persons, and the angels that sinned will be judged in the end. **God at times uses evil and wicked men, angels and spirits to do what must be done. In the Old Testament, when Israel would backslide, many times God would allow enemies to invade the land to bring the people back to him in worship and praise.** J. Narver Gortner writes, "The four angels which were bound at sometime in the past in the great river Euphrates, and are still bound there, are judgment angels, and at the appointed time for which they are being held, will be loosed."

And in Verse 15, the same four angels are loosed for an hour and a day and a month and a year, for to slay the third part of men. **One thing we must remember is that the events in chapters 7-11 are parenthetical, which means what? That they are not in chronological order but are happening at the same times as other events are taking place.** These four angels are given a set time to do their assigned task, to kill one third of the

114

world's population. They are given 13 months and one day and one hour. In Verse 16, we see that these four angels raise an army of horsemen (spiritual beings; evil spirits), and the number of these horsemen is two hundred thousand thousand (200,000,000). John goes on in Verse 17 to tell what he saw in a vision. He says horses and them that sat upon the horses, and he speaks of the horses as having heads like lions, and out of their mouths issued fire and smoke and brimstone. In the eighteenth verse, it states that **by these three was the third part of men killed by fire, by smoke and by brimstone that came out of their mouths and in their tails**.

In Verse 20, we read of men's continued folly, because **after all of these things, men still refuse to repent and accept Jesus Christ as their Savior; they continue to worship the works of their hands.** One third of what was left of man after the seals were opened is now dead. Oh, the hardness that a man's heart can reach. Verse 20 tells us: *"Neither repented they of their murders, nor of their sorceries, not of their fornication, not of their thefts."* What more can we say? **Man has reached the place where he worships the creature more than the creator.** His heart has become so hardened that he would rather die than confess his failures and ask for mercy. Man's stubbornness has always been one of his greatest faults. Man would rather go into eternity lost without God than admit he is wrong about being a sinner.

Chapter 9 Review Questions

1. What was given to the star that fell to the earth?

_____

_____

2. What comes out of the bottomless pit, and what is their purpose?_____

_____

3. What do men seek and cannot find it because it flees from them? _____

4. What is the name of the king over the locust in Hebrew and in Greek? _____

_____

5. From where on the golden altar does the voice come?

_____

_____

6. How long were these four evil angels to be loosed?

_____

7. What was the purpose of these four angels?

_____

_____

8. What must we remember about chapters 7-10?

_____

_____

9. What part of mankind were killed during this time period?

_____

10. After all that happened, what did man still not do?

_____

_____

Chapter 10

Revelation 10:1-7

[1] And I saw another mighty angel come down from heaven, clothed with a cloud: and a rainbow was upon his head, and his face was as it were the sun, and his feet as pillars of fire:

[2] And he had in his hand a little book open: and he set his right foot upon the sea, and his left foot on the earth,

[3] And cried with a loud voice, as when a lion roareth: and when he had cried, seven thunders uttered their voices.

[4] And when the seven thunders had uttered their voices, I was about to write: and I heard a voice from heaven saying unto me, Seal up those things which the seven thunders uttered, and write them not.

[5] And the angel which I saw stand upon the sea and upon the earth lifted up his hand to heaven,

[6] And sware by him that liveth for ever and ever, who created heaven, and the things that therein are, and the earth, and the things that therein are, and the sea, and the things which are therein, that there should be time no longer:

[7] But in the days of the voice of the seventh angel, when he shall begin to sound, the mystery of God should be finished, as he hath declared to his servants the prophets.

Here John *"saw another mighty angel come down from heaven, clothed with a cloud, and a rainbow was upon his head, and his face was as it were the sun and his feet as pillars of fire."* **General consensus is that this mighty angel is the son of God, Jesus Christ, himself.** This angel had in his hand a little book open, and he set his right foot upon the sea, and his left foot on the earth. *Prevision of History* refers to Jesus being the angel. "The inner circle of Christ's apostles, Peter, James, and John, beheld Jesus the Son of God transfigured and 'his face did shine as the sun.' No portrayal like this can be attributed to a created angel." Remember, all of this takes place between the opening of the sixth and seventh seals. **We must keep in mind that Revelation isn't written in chronological order, and many of the events in this book take place at the same time.** There's only speculation as to what the little book contained; it's not for us to know. John hears a loud voice, and then seven thunders utter their voices. John was about to write when he heard a voice from heaven telling him *"to seal up those things which the seven thunders uttered"* and not to write about it. We aren't to know what takes place at this point. Some things must remain secret. Verse 5 states that the angel, which is believed to be Christ, lifted up his hand to heaven. In Verse 6, the angel swore by him that lives forever and ever, the one which created the heavens, the earth and the sea and that there should be time no longer. **This is misleading, since we know that the thousand-year reign of peace is still to come. I believe He's talking about the end of the tribulation period which is shortly to come to an end, because in the next verse, we are talking about the days of the voice of the seventh angel.** This is why part of this chapter is parenthetical, in other words, it's in the wrong place to be in chronological (not in proper) order. The seventh trumpet hasn't sounded, but **when it begins to sound, the mystery of God should be finished, as he hath declared to his servants, the prophets**.

Revelation 10:8-11

⁸ And the voice which I heard from heaven spake unto me again, and said, Go and take the little book which is open in the hand of the angel which standeth upon the sea and upon the earth.
⁹ And I went unto the angel, and said unto him, Give me the little book. And he said unto me, Take it, and eat it up; and it shall make thy belly bitter, but it shall be in thy mouth sweet as honey.
¹⁰ And I took the little book out of the angel's hand, and ate it up; and it was in my mouth sweet as honey: and as soon as I had eaten it, my belly was bitter.
¹¹ And he said unto me, Thou must prophesy again before many peoples, and nations, and tongues, and kings.

The voice that John heard spoke again and told John to go and take the little book which is open in the hand of the angel. John then went to the angel, asked for the little book, and was told by the angel to take the book and to eat it up. The book would make his belly bitter, but that it would be sweet in his mouth, as sweet as honey. **Why sweet and then bitter? Could it be that as we get saved, the joy of God's spirit and the sweetness of His presence is so wonderful, because His Word contains the words of life. But then we begin to think about those who aren't saved and who'll miss the rapture, and as we begin to grieve, bitterness comes as we mourn for the lost.**

We must consider that the Bible is God's inspired word. It behooves us to study it, to digest it so that it becomes a part of us, so that it feeds our spiritual man, and we grow spiritually stronger by it. The studying of God's Word has a two-fold effect upon us: it gives us joy in serving our Lord, but at the same time, it gives us sadness or bitterness when we consider the lost souls that will miss the glory of heaven. John was told that he must prophesy against many nations, peoples, and tongues, which he did in obeying God's word. John has gone to heaven, but we are left to carry on the message that there is a heaven to gain and a hell to shun.

Chapter 10 Review Questions

1. Who is this mighty angel believed to be?

_____

2. What does he hold in his hand?

_____

_____

3. What was John told not to write?

_____

_____

4. What was John told to do with the little book?

_____

_____

5. In the last verse, what is John told that he must do?

_____

_____

6. Why should we carry on John's message today?

_____

Chapter 11

Revelation 11:1-2

¹ And there was given me a reed like unto a rod: and the angel stood, saying, Rise, and measure the temple of God, and the altar, and them that worship therein.
² But the court which is without the temple leave out, and measure it not; for it is given unto the Gentiles: and the holy city shall they tread under foot forty and two months.

John was given a reed which was like a rod, and the angel told John to rise up and to measure the temple of God, the altar and them that worship therein. **This measuring of the temple isn't one of the temples built in the past but will be the new temple that Israel is preparing to build in the very near future.** Why John is told to measure it isn't clear.

The outer court, in Verse 2, John is told not to measure, because it's given unto the Gentiles. And the holy city shall they tread underfoot for forty-two months. **For the temple to be rebuilt, Israel must have possession of the temple mount or the permission of the temple mount authority. Will the Mosque of Omar be torn down, or will the new temple be built beside it, as some say that it can be? The answer to these questions aren't given, but the temple will be rebuilt.** Jerusalem will be trodden underfoot (they will walk all over it) for forty-two months, which equals three-and-a-half years. These three-and-a-half years will correspond to the last three-and-a-half years of the tribulation period. During this time, the Jews will witness the abomination of desolation.

Dr. Williams, in *Prevision of History*, wrote: "What is the abomination of desolation? Paul received this revelation of the coming of the man of sin, the son of perdition who would set himself up as God in the temple of God. [2 Thessalonians 2:3-4 – *³ Let no man deceive you by any means: for that day shall not come, except there come a falling away first, and that man of sin be revealed, the son of perdition; ⁴ Who opposeth and exalteth himself above all that is called God, or that is worshipped; so that he as God sitteth in the temple of God, shewing himself that he is God.*] John's prevision of the beast of Revelation 13:5 coincides with the same period. 'Forty-two months' is the time allowed the satanically empowered antichrist to have world domination. He will demand worship and compulsory taking of his mark and number. In cooperation with the Second Beast of Revelation 13:11 (the False Prophet) an image is to be erected, and to this image all must bow. The Jews cannot worship a man who demands the breaking of the cardinal law of the Ten Commandments. This will be the abomination of desolation. The covenant made with them will be broken 'in the midst (middle) of the week.' Then the horrible wrath of the devil will be poured out on the woman, (National Israel), who will flee into the wilderness prepared for her to abide 1,260 days as found in Revelation 12:6; which again is expressed as time (one year) time (two years), and half time (one half year) in Revelation 12:14. This is the same time concerning which Christ warned His disciples in His Olivet discourse." Matthew 24:15-22 warns us: "*When ye therefore shall*

see the abomination of desolation, spoken of by Daniel the proph-
et, stand in the holy place, (whoso readeth, let him understand:)
Then let them which be in Judaea flee into the mountains: Let him
which is on the housetop not come down to take any thing out of
his house: Neither let him which is in the field return back to take
his clothes. And woe unto them that are with child, and to them
that give suck in those days! But pray ye that your flight be not in
the winter, neither on the sabbath day: For then shall be great
tribulation, such as was not since the beginning of the world to
this time, no, nor ever shall be. And except those days should be
shortened, there should no flesh be saved: but for the elect's sake
those days shall be shortened."

Jesus warned His disciples in Matthew that these things would come to pass. **The disciples may not have truly understood what Jesus meant at that time, but now with Revelation before us, we can see and partially understand what the scriptures are saying to us.** *"He that hath an ear to hear let him hear what the spirit is saying unto the churches."*

Revelation 11:3-14

[3] And I will give power unto my two witnesses, and they shall prophesy a thousand two hundred and threescore days, clothed in sackcloth.
[4] These are the two olive trees, and the two candlesticks standing before the God of the earth.
[5] And if any man will hurt them, fire proceedeth out of their mouth, and devoureth their enemies: and if any man will hurt them, he must in this manner be killed.
[6] These have power to shut heaven, that it rain not in the days of their prophecy: and have power over waters to

turn them to blood, and to smite the earth with all plagues, as often as they will.

⁷ And when they shall have finished their testimony, the beast that ascendeth out of the bottomless pit shall make war against them, and shall overcome them, and kill them.

⁸ And their dead bodies shall lie in the street of the great city, which spiritually is called Sodom and Egypt, where also our Lord was crucified.

⁹ And they of the people and kindreds and tongues and nations shall see their dead bodies three days and an half, and shall not suffer their dead bodies to be put in graves.

¹⁰ And they that dwell upon the earth shall rejoice over them, and make merry, and shall send gifts one to another; because these two prophets tormented them that dwelt on the earth.

¹¹ And after three days and an half the Spirit of life from God entered into them, and they stood upon their feet; and great fear fell upon them which saw them.

¹² And they heard a great voice from heaven saying unto them, Come up hither. And they ascended up to heaven in a cloud; and their enemies beheld them.

¹³ And the same hour was there a great earthquake, and the tenth part of the city fell, and in the earthquake were slain of men seven thousand: and the remnant were affrighted, and gave glory to the God of heaven.

¹⁴ The second woe is past; and, behold, the third woe cometh quickly.

"And I will give power unto my two witnesses, and they shall prophesy a thousand two hundred and threescore days," means that **they will prophesy for the same time frame that Je-**

rusalem is overrun with the Gentiles. For three-and-a-half years they will prophesy of God and His power. **At the end of this time they will be killed, but not till the end of the time God has allowed for them.** They are described in Verse 4 as *"two olive trees, and the two candlesticks standing before the God of the earth."*

Who are these two witnesses? There are some who say that they are Moses and Elijah. John Phillips, in *Exploring Revelation,* states: "There has been much speculation about the identity of these two men. One of them is probably Elijah. Fire was characteristic of his ministry, and his miracles were frequently those of judgment. Some think the other witness might be Moses for, he, like Elijah, was a representative man. Between them they stood for the Old Testament ministry, 'the law and the prophets.' Together they stood with the Lord on the mount of transfiguration. But since both these witnesses are to be executed by the beast, the case for Moses is weakened. Moses has already died, and it is appointed unto men once to die. [Hebrews 9:27 – *And as it is appointed unto men once to die, but after this the judgment*:] Some think the second witness is Enoch. Enoch, like Elijah, was a lonely voice for God in an apostate age, and again like Elijah, he was caught up living into heaven without passing through the article of death."

I like to believe the two witnesses are Enoch and Elijah; both men were taken into heaven without dying. One wonders what special fellowship these men must have had with God. Genesis 5:24 tells us: *"And Enoch walked with God: and he was not; for God took him."* We know that Adam and Eve walked with God in the cool of the evening before they sinned and were cast out of the garden. But here we read that Enoch walked with God. Could it be that Enoch found that fellowship that Adam and Eve sadly threw away? That he walked with God literally and then was not, for God took him to heaven to be with Him? We know the story of Elijah and the fiery chariot and how God took him to heaven.

These two men aren't known to us, for God doesn't give us their names. We must settle for our own opinion. But God chose them for this certain time. Zechariah 4:11-14 states: *"Then answered I, and said unto him, What are these two olive trees upon the right side of the candlestick and upon the left side thereof? And I answered again, and said unto him, What be these two olive branches which through the two golden pipes empty the golden oil out of themselves? And he answered me and said, Knowest thou not what these be? And I said, No, my lord. Then said he, These are the two anointed ones, that stand by the Lord of the whole earth."* Here, in Zechariah, the Lord gives us a preview of these two witnesses. Given the time to truly study, it's amazing what scripture reveals. The meaning of what God allowed Zechariah to see in the days of the Old Testament, He also reveals in the New Testament.

We get further insight in Verse 5 that these witnesses have a job to perform. If any man tries to hurt them, **fire will proceed out of their mouths and destroy those who would hinder their work for the Lord**. This is according to scripture, the only way that their enemies will be killed. These witnesses also have powers that are described in Verse 6. Their power to **cause the rain to stop** means that it doesn't rain in the days of their prophecy, three-and-one-half without rain. They have the power to **turn water into blood and to smite the earth with all plagues** as often as they will.

In Verses 7-8 we read what happens to them. At the end of their ministry, **the beast that cometh out of the bottomless pit**

will make war against the witnesses, shall overcome them and kill them. Then their dead bodies shall lay in the street of the great city (Jerusalem, which spiritually is called Sodom and Egypt) where our Lord and Savior was crucified. Verses 9-10 tell us that all the people of the world will see their dead bodies lying in the street. For three-and-a-half days they will lay dead. Their bodies will not be laid in graves but left where they were killed. **The whole earth will rejoice because they are dead. It will be like Christmas, they will send gifts to one another, and there will be one worldwide party, but the end is not yet come.** Then after three and a half days, according to Verse 11, the Spirit of life from God entered into them, and they stood upon their feet, and great fear fell upon them which saw them. In this age of electronics, (the computer, television and instant communication) it will be easy for the whole world to see these men die. The world will think that they have won a great victory. How wrong they'll be, for three-and-a-half days they laid in the street. **But at the appointed time, God will give them back the Spirit of life, and they will stand to their feet.** Instant communication allows the world to know in a matter of minutes, and a great fear will fall upon people; the party will be over; so much for the Devil's short lived victory. Then in Verses 12-13, we read where a great voice was heard from heaven saying unto them, "Come up hither," and they rose up into heaven in a cloud, and the world will see it all and fear. And in that hour, there was a great earthquake, and one-tenth of the city was destroyed, and seven thousand men died in the earthquake. **After all this had happened, there came upon the remnant that was left a great fear. And according to John, they gave glory to God.** It is my opinion that those who gave glory to God are the remnant of the Jews, although the scriptures do not give us any information on this.

A strong warning is given to us in Verse 14. *"Two woes are past and the third is yet to come and it will come quickly."*

Revelation 11:15-19

[15] And the seventh angel sounded; and there were great voices in heaven, saying, The kingdoms of this world are become the kingdoms of our Lord, and of his Christ; and he shall reign for ever and ever.
[16] And the four and twenty elders, which sat before God on their seats, fell upon their faces, and worshipped God,
[17] Saying, We give thee thanks, O Lord God Almighty, which art, and wast, and art to come; because thou hast taken to thee thy great power, and hast reigned.
[18] And the nations were angry, and thy wrath is come, and the time of the dead, that they should be judged, and that thou shouldest give reward unto thy servants the prophets, and to the saints, and them that fear thy name, small and great; and shouldest destroy them which destroy the earth.
[19] And the temple of God was opened in heaven, and there was seen in his temple the ark of his testament: and there were lightnings, and voices, and thunderings, and an earthquake, and great hail.

"And the seventh angel sounded; and there were great voices in heaven, saying, The kingdoms of this world are become the kingdoms of our Lord, and of his Christ; and he shall reign for ever and ever." **Heaven is rejoicing because Christ is soon to set up his kingdom on the earth.** Then in Verse 16 we read about the twenty-four elders which are before the throne of God who fall upon their faces and worship and give glory and praise to

132

Almighty God. It continues in Verse 17 about the elders, as they praise God. Which is, and was, and is to come, for His reigning power. Verse 18 states that the nations were angry, but the time of God's wrath is come upon the world; for there is much more to come. **The time has come that the martyrs who gave their lives for God and Christ should be judged, that rewards should be handed out to God's servants, the prophets and to the saints, and to all who fear the name of Almighty God, both small and great, that those who destroyed the earth should also be destroyed.**

Verse 19 starts out by saying that the temple of God was opened in heaven. The ark of his testament is seen in the temple of God, and there *"was lightnings, and voices, and thunderings, and an earthquake, and great hail."*

There are many Bible scholars who believe that this is the Ark of the Covenant that has been transported to heaven. However, I do not believe this to be so. We need to remember that the Ark of the Covenant was made by man; God gave the instructions to Moses for its making, and it was made to be a copy of the Golden Ark that is before the throne. The ark that was in the Holy of Holies in the tabernacle, and later in the temple in Jerusalem, is in a hiding place waiting for the temple to be built again in Jerusalem. The Jewish priests are now in training to offer animal sacrifices again when the new temple is completed. However, we know that the blood of animals cannot take away the sins of man.

Chapter 11 Review Questions

1. What temple is John told to measure?

_____

2. Why is John told not to measure the outer court?

_____

_____

3. Who are the two witnesses believed to be?

_____

_____

4. What is the "abomination of desolation"?

_____

_____

_____

5. The two witnesses whose bodies have lain in the streets for three-and-one-half days shall do what?

_____

_____

6. In Verse 18 we read that the time has come to judge the dead. Who are these dead?

_____

_____

7. What was seen when the temple of God was opened in heaven?_____

_____

Chapter 12

Revelation 12:1-6

[1] And there appeared a great wonder in heaven; a woman clothed with the sun, and the moon under her feet, and upon her head a crown of twelve stars:

[2] And she being with child cried, travailing in birth, and pained to be delivered.

[3] And there appeared another wonder in heaven; and behold a great red dragon, having seven heads and ten horns, and seven crowns upon his heads.

[4] And his tail drew the third part of the stars of heaven, and did cast them to the earth: and the dragon stood before the woman which was ready to be delivered, for to devour her child as soon as it was born.

[5] And she brought forth a man child, who was to rule all nations with a rod of iron: and her child was caught up unto God, and to his throne.

[6] And the woman fled into the wilderness, where she hath a place prepared of God, that they should feed her there a thousand two hundred and threescore days.

Remember that Chapter 12 is parenthetical, which means that these verses are not in chronological order, and they could have already happened or could happen anywhere in the book of Revelation.

Verse 1 begins with a great wonder or sign appearing in heaven, a sun-clothed woman. Who can this woman be? This woman can only be a symbolized Israel. **The twelve stars are a symbol of the twelve tribes of Israel.** Then, in Verse 2, the travailing of the woman (Israel) is shown here as about to give birth. **If we look at Israel, we know that from the time of Malachi to John the Baptist, there wasn't a prophet's voice heard in Israel for a period of about four hundred years. Israel was praying for their Messiah to come and set them free from their oppressors; they were in travail.** According to John Phillips in *Exploring Revelation,* "This takes us back to the story of Joseph in Genesis 37. The only scripture that bears any correspondence with this sign, Joseph dreamed that the sun, the moon, and the eleven stars made obeisance to him. He understood from this that his parents and his brethren would bow down to him. His dream was a revelation from God that Israel would be preserved through him." **Israel gave us that Son who is now in heaven. His name is Jesus, the Christ.**

Verse 3 tells us that there appeared another wonder (or sign) in heaven. *"Behold a great red dragon, having seven heads and ten horns and seven crowns upon his heads."* Who is this dragon? We find the answer farther down in Verse 9. The dragon is Satan, that old dragon, the devil. Verse 4 gives us more information about the devil and what he did. The Word says that his tail drew one third of the stars (angels) from heaven and cast them to the earth. **There can be found no sin in heaven.** The scripture states: *"If God spared not the angels that sinned"* (2 Peter 2:4). The story of Satan's fall is recorded in scripture, if we take the time to search it out.

1. God-anointed Cherub: Ezekiel 28:12-17 – *12 Son of man, take up a lamentation upon the king of Tyrus, and say unto him, Thus saith the Lord GOD; Thou sealest up the sum, full of wisdom, and perfect in beauty. 13 Thou hast been in Eden the garden of God; every precious stone was thy covering, the sardius, topaz, and the diamond, the beryl, the onyx, and the jasper, the sapphire, the emerald, and the carbuncle, and gold: the workmanship of thy tabrets and of thy pipes was prepared in thee in the day that thou wast created. 14 Thou art the anointed cherub that covereth; and I have set thee so: thou wast upon the holy mountain of God; thou hast walked up and down in the midst of the stones of fire. 15 Thou wast perfect in thy ways from the day that thou wast created, till iniquity was found in thee. 16 By the multitude of thy merchandise they have filled the midst of thee with violence, and thou hast sinned: therefore I will cast thee as profane out of the mountain of God: and I will destroy thee, O covering cherub, from the midst of the stones of fire. 17 Thine heart was lifted up because of thy beauty, thou hast corrupted thy wisdom by reason of thy brightness: I will cast thee to the ground, I will lay thee before kings, that they may behold thee.*

2. How art thou fallen from heaven, O Lucifer: Isaiah 14:12-14 – *12 How art thou fallen from heaven, O Lucifer, son of the morning! how art thou cut down to the ground, which didst weaken the nations! 13 For thou hast said in thine heart, I will ascend into heaven, I will exalt my throne above the stars of God: I will sit*

also upon the mount of the congregation, in the sides of the north: ¹⁴ I will ascend above the heights of the clouds; I will be like the most High.

The rest of Verse 4 tells us **it was Satan's plan to destroy Jesus as soon as he was born, but we know this plan failed.** Many innocent children died, as Herod tried to kill the Christ child. God had forewarned Joseph in a dream to flee into Egypt, in accordance with scripture that said, *"out of Egypt have I called my son."*

Revelation 12:5 tells us, *"And she brought forth a man child, who was to rule all nations with a rod of iron: and her child was caught up unto God, and to his throne."* Scripture states that Jesus is seated at the right hand of God. Then in Verse 6, it states that the woman (the nation of Israel) fled into the wilderness where God has a place prepared for her to hide. **There she will be for one thousand, two hundred, and three score days, or three-and-one-half years, according to the plan of God.**

Revelation 12:7-12

⁷ And there was war in heaven: Michael and his angels fought against the dragon; and the dragon fought and his angels,
⁸ And prevailed not; neither was their place found any more in heaven.
⁹ And the great dragon was cast out, that old serpent, called the Devil, and Satan, which deceiveth the whole world: he was cast out into the earth, and his angels were cast out with him.
¹⁰ And I heard a loud voice saying in heaven, Now is come

salvation, and strength, and the kingdom of our God, and the power of his Christ: for the accuser of our brethren is cast down, which accused them before our God day and night.

[11] And they overcame him by the blood of the Lamb, and by the word of their testimony; and they loved not their lives unto the death.

[12] Therefore rejoice, ye heavens, and ye that dwell in them. Woe to the inhabiters of the earth and of the sea! for the devil is come down unto you, having great wrath, because he knoweth that he hath but a short time.

Starting with Verse 7, we begin to read about a great war that takes place in heaven. **The war is fought between Michael and his angels and Satan, that old dragon and his angels.** In Verse 8, Satan was defeated, and there was no place in heaven found for him. Verse 9 tells that the great dragon (the devil, Satan, the deceiver of the whole earth) was cast out, he and all of his angels. He, Satan, and all of his angels were cast into the earth. One important question: When did or does this take place? There are those that believe that all of what we have read in Chapter 12 has yet to take place; in other words, they say that Satan is still in heaven, he and his angels have not yet been cast out, and that the war between Michael and Satan has not yet happened. **This is not so. The scriptures in Ezekiel and Isaiah aren't prophesies of things yet to come, but are of things that have already happened.** Too much scripture shows this war has already happened, and that Satan has already been cast out of heaven. In 2 Peter 2:4, we read, *"For if God spared not the angels that sinned, but cast them down to hell, and delivered them into chains of darkness, to be reserved unto judgment."* **This is spoken in the past tense,**

which means it has already taken place. Ezekiel and Isaiah also speak in the past tense of things that have already happened. In 2 Peter 2:4, we find, "*⁴ For if God spared not the angels that sinned, but cast them down to hell, and delivered them into chains of darkness, to be reserved unto judgment;*" **We read about the angels which kept not their first estate, but left their own habitation, and are now reserved in everlasting chains and waiting for the judgment. This is past tense; it's already happened.**

God reveals that Satan has already been cast out of heaven, along with his angels. **What John is seeing is the whole plan of God from beginning to end, from the war that took place in heaven, to Adam and Eve's fall, to what will take place in the future.** What John saw he wrote in a book; he wrote in segments as he saw what was going on. For example, the woman, the child, Israel and the birth of Jesus, all of these things had already taken place. Jesus went to the cross in about 33 A.D. while John wrote Revelation somewhere around 95 A.D., according to Bible scholars. **So, these things had already come to pass, before John began to write Revelation; this is why it's so easy to become confused in Revelation.**

Next John tells of a loud voice saying, "*Now is come salvation, and strength, and the kingdom of our God . . . for the accuser of our brethren is cast down . . . And they overcame him by the blood of the Lamb, and by the word of their testimony.*" **This is our victory covered by the blood, sins washed away, and a testimony of what God has done and what He is going to do by His mighty power.**

Revelation 12:12 says, "*Therefore rejoice, ye heavens, and ye that dwell in them.*" We are told there's to be a time of rejoicing in heaven, because the war in heaven's over, the victory won and **Satan and his horde were cast down to earth. Woe to** the people of earth because the devil is angry. Satan knows that he only has a short time to work against God before the final end.

Revelation 12:13-17

13 And when the dragon saw that he was cast unto the earth, he persecuted the woman which brought forth the man child.
14 And to the woman were given two wings of a great eagle, that she might fly into the wilderness, into her place, where she is nourished for a time, and times, and half a time, from the face of the serpent.
15 And the serpent cast out of his mouth water as a flood after the woman, that he might cause her to be carried away of the flood.
16 And the earth helped the woman, and the earth opened her mouth, and swallowed up the flood which the dragon cast out of his mouth.
17 And the dragon was wroth with the woman, and went to make war with the remnant of her seed, which keep the commandments of God, and have the testimony of Jesus Christ.

John Phillips best explains these verses: "As Israel in ancient times fled into the wilderness (Exodus 15:5), so in a future day will she flee again. The Lord Jesus spoke of this flight in His Olivet discourse. *'Pray,'* He said, *"that your flight be not in the winter, neither on the Sabbath day"* (Matthew 24:20). Israel's plight will be desperate, but even so God will raise up among the Gentiles those who will render help. They will shield and shelter the Jews at great personal risk and will be numbered among the sheep at the judgment of the living nations when the Lord returns (Matthew 25:31-46). But Israel's chief hiding place will be in what is called here 'the wilderness.' The greatest flight will be from Jerusalem and the land of Israel, the focal point of the beast's hatred, and God will repeat His former miracles and furnish for His beloved refugees a table in the wilderness." **Again we see how long Israel will be in the wilderness, three-and-one-half years.**

In Verse 15 we read that the devil cast out of his mouth water as a flood. This is a metaphor. **In the pages of the Bible we read many times about enemy armies that came as a flood, so what is meant here is that the devil sent armies or soldiers after the Jews.** Verse 16 tells us that the earth helped the Jews, that **the earth opened up and swallowed the enemies of God's chosen people. We have record of this happening at another time. In Numbers, we read about Korah, Dathan and Abiram and how they perished.** [Numbers 16:26-34 – *26 And he spake unto the congregation, saying, Depart, I pray you, from the tents of these wicked men, and touch nothing of theirs, lest ye be consumed in all their sins. 27 So they gat up from the tabernacle of Korah, Dathan, and Abiram, on every side: and Dathan and Abiram came out, and stood in the door of their tents, and their wives, and their sons, and their little children. 28 And Moses said, Hereby ye shall know that the LORD hath sent me to do all these works; for I have not done them of mine own mind. 29 If these men die the common death of all men, or if they be visited after the visitation of all men; then the LORD hath not sent me. 30 But if the LORD make a new thing, and the earth open her mouth, and swallow them up, with all that appertain unto them, and they go down quick into the pit; then ye shall understand that these men* *have provoked the LORD. ³¹ And it came to pass, as he had made an end of speaking all these words, that the ground clave asunder that was under them: ³² And the earth opened her mouth, and swallowed them up, and their houses, and all the men that appertained unto Korah, and all their goods. ³³ They, and all that appertained to them, went down alive into the pit, and the earth closed upon them: and they perished from among the congregation. ³⁴ And all Israel that were round about them fled at the cry of them: for they said, Lest the earth swallow us up also.]*

The last verse in this chapter is very self-explaining. The devil was angry that God had stopped his plans. So, to get revenge, the devil would make war against the remnant of the Jews that was left. **These are the Jews that keep the commandments of God, the ones who have accepted Jesus as their Savior, and have kept their testimony of Jesus Christ.**

Chapter 12 Review Questions

1. When events are not in chronological order, they are called what? _____

2. Who is the sun-clothed woman?

_____

3. Who is this man-child that the woman brought forth?

_____

4. Who is the dragon?

_____

5. How many of the angels were cast out of heaven?

_____

6. How long will Israel be in the wilderness?

_____

7. What is the meaning of the phrase, *"the serpent cast out of his mouth water as a flood,"* **which is found in Verse 15?**

_____

_____

8. Where else does the Bible speak of the earth opening up?

_____

Chapter 13

Revelation 13:1-10

¹ And I stood upon the sand of the sea, and saw a beast rise up out of the sea, having seven heads and ten horns, and upon his horns ten crowns, and upon his heads the name of blasphemy.
² And the beast which I saw was like unto a leopard, and his feet were as the feet of a bear, and his mouth as the mouth of a lion: and the dragon gave him his power, and his seat, and great authority.
³ And I saw one of his heads as it were wounded to death; and his deadly wound was healed: and all the world wondered after the beast.
⁴ And they worshipped the dragon which gave power unto the beast: and they worshipped the beast, saying, Who is like unto the beast? who is able to make war with him?
⁵ And there was given unto him a mouth speaking great things and blasphemies; and power was given unto him to continue forty and two months.
⁶ And he opened his mouth in blasphemy against God, to blaspheme his name, and his tabernacle, and them that dwell in heaven.
⁷ And it was given unto him to make war with the saints,

and to overcome them: and power was given him over all
kindreds, and tongues, and nations.
⁸ And all that dwell upon the earth shall worship him,
whose names are not written in the book of life of the
Lamb slain from the foundation of the world.
⁹ If any man have an ear, let him hear.
¹⁰ He that leadeth into captivity shall go into captivity: he
that killeth with the sword must be killed with the sword.
Here is the patience and the faith of the saints.

John is giving us a picture of what he's viewing. (Remember, the things that take place in Revelation take place literally, symbolically and figuratively.) John saw a beast rise up out of the sea. **The sea that John speaks of here is not a sea of water, but a sea of masses of people. The antichrist will come from among the people.** Here, the sea is figurative, relating to people. The beast had seven heads and ten horns which symbolize the last great empires of the Gentiles. Dr. Williams states: "The Mystery of Iniquity will have full sway. Because men have loved the lie and have refused to repent, God will send them strong delusions. They will believe this lie, the devil's masterpiece of delusion leading to the worship of the devil and the beast."

In Verse 2, the beast which John saw was a man. **The symbols which John saw, the leopard, the feet of a bear and the mouth of a lion, are great, evil empires, which show us how evil this "Man of Sin" will be.**

2 Thessalonians 2:3-4

³ Let no man deceive you by any means: for that day shall
not come, except there come a falling away first, and that

150

man of sin be revealed, the son of perdition;
⁴ Who opposeth and exalteth himself above all that is called God, or that is worshipped; so that he as God sitteth in the temple of God, shewing himself that he is God.

Also, in this same verse, the antichrist is called the son of perdition. In Arthur Pink's book *The Antichrist*, he lists the names the Bible gives to the antichrist, where they are found and some explanations for each. The antichrist is a very real person, and he is given great power and authority by the dragon, the old devil.

"And I saw one of his heads as it were wounded to death; and his deadly wound was healed." (Revelation 13:3) In *Prevision of History*, Dr. Williams made a statement that I whole heartedly agree with. She wrote, "Let it be stated and acknowledged forever there is only One who can make this affirmation, 'I am the resurrection and the life.' (John 11:25) He gave His life and declared Himself the Son of God by His resurrection." As we read the verse closely, we will see the scripture states as *"it were wounded to death,"* and his deadly wound was healed. The seven heads of the beast are symbolic. The beast is described more in Revelation 17:8-11, where scripture states that the seven heads are seven hills. This brings to mind Rome, the city built on seven hills. Another interpretation is presented by Finis Jennings Dake, who states "that these seven heads referred to kings and kingdoms which would constitute the times of the Gentiles ruling over Israel. Delving back into history from the time of John, the five Gentile empires which had ruled Israel were Egypt, Assyria, Babylonia, Medo-Persia, and Greece, and the empire at the time of John was Rome. The seventh future empire would therefore be the revised and revived Holy Roman Empire, thus, the antichrist's

world empire would be the seventh." Whatever view you accept, **it's evident that the antichrist will inherit all of the Gentile authority and power and will rule the world**. Then Verse 4 states that the people of the world will worship the dragon, who gave power to the beast, and they also will worship the beast.

There was given to the beast (Verses 5-6) great power, and he spoke great things and blasphemies for the space of 42 months (three-and-one-half years). **The beast opened his mouth in blasphemy of God, to blaspheme the name of God, his tabernacle and all that dwell in heaven. And it was given unto him to make war with the saints, those who know what's taking place and have made up their minds that they will stand for God and Jesus Christ regardless of the price.** Verse 7 suggests it's the only way for them to make heaven their home.

We find in verses 8-10 that all the people that dwell upon the earth, whose names are not written in the Lamb's Book of Life, will worship the antichrist. If any man *"have an ear [to hear], let him hear."* **He that killeth with the sword must be killed with the sword. Herein is the patience and the faith of the saints.** John Phillips writes: "Groups of God's people are no longer in focus: it has come down to individuals now, one here, one there will stand out against the rising floodtide of popular enthusiasm and religious fervor for the beast. Captivity, execution, torture await the faithful; patience and faith will be needed. There will be those who will respond."

Revelation 13:11-18

[11] And I beheld another beast coming up out of the earth; and he had two horns like a lamb, and he spake as a dragon.

12 And he exerciseth all the power of the first beast before him, and causeth the earth and them which dwell therein to worship the first beast, whose deadly wound was healed.

13 And he doeth great wonders, so that he maketh fire come down from heaven on the earth in the sight of men,

14 And deceiveth them that dwell on the earth by the means of those miracles which he had power to do in the sight of the beast; saying to them that dwell on the earth, that they should make an image to the beast, which had the wound by a sword, and did live.

15 And he had power to give life unto the image of the beast, that the image of the beast should both speak, and cause that as many as would not worship the image of the beast should be killed.

16 And he causeth all, both small and great, rich and poor, free and bond, to receive a mark in their right hand, or in their foreheads:

17 And that no man might buy or sell, save he that had the mark, or the name of the beast, or the number of his name.

18 Here is wisdom. Let him that hath understanding count the number of the beast: for it is the number of a man; and his number is Six hundred threescore and six.

What John saw next (Verse 11) was another beast coming up out of the earth, and he had two horns like a lamb, but he spoke like a dragon. Who is this beast? He's the false prophet. He comes as a lamb, but lambs don't have horns. **The false prophet's work is to cause everyone on the earth to worship the antichrist.** This false prophet will do great wonders and show great signs, even calling fire down from heaven, but he's still the servant of the devil. For everything that God has, the devil has a counterfeit. When Moses and Aaron stood before Pharaoh, Pharaoh demanded a miracle. God commanded them to show him a miracle by Aaron casting his rod down before Pharaoh, and the rod became a serpent. Pharaoh then called in his wise men and sorcerers, and the magicians in like manner cast down their rods, and they also became serpents. But, **God is greater than the forces of the devil, and Aaron's rod swallowed up the rods of the magicians**.

Exodus 7:8-12

> *[8] And the LORD spake unto Moses and unto Aaron, saying,*
>
> *[9] When Pharaoh shall speak unto you, saying, Shew a miracle for you: then thou shalt say unto Aaron, Take thy rod, and cast it before Pharaoh, and it shall become a serpent.*
>
> *[10] And Moses and Aaron went in unto Pharaoh, and they did so as the LORD had commanded: and Aaron cast down his rod before Pharaoh, and before his servants, and it became a serpent.*
>
> *[11] Then Pharaoh also called the wise men and the sorcerers: now the magicians of Egypt, they also did in like manner with their enchantments.*
>
> *[12] For they cast down every man his rod, and they became serpents: but Aaron's rod swallowed up their rods.*

We cannot afford to let the devil trick us by false signs and wonders. We must know the Word so that we won't be

fooled by the enemy of our souls. Verses 14-15 speak of those signs and miracles, and the false prophet commands an image be made of the antichrist. When this image is completed, the people are commanded to worship it, and all who would not worship the image were killed. So great will be the force of evil that the false prophet will even make the image to appear to come to life and to speak. **Man will believe his false miracle and will fall into line in the devil's plan.**

Verses 16-17 again speak of the false prophet, and this time he will cause all – small and great, rich and poor, free and bond – to receive a mark in their right hand or in their forehead. Without this mark, no one can buy or sell anything, except those who have the mark, or the name of the beast, or the number of his name. We are given a warning: Revelation 13:18 tell us, *"Here is wisdom. Let him that hath understanding count the number of the beast: for it is the number of a man; and his number is Six hundred threescore and six."* **No one knows what this mark will be, but one thing is for sure, there will be a mark of some kind, and without it you can neither buy nor sell, and this mark will be put onto or in the body.**

Chapter 13 Review Questions

1. The things that take place in Revelation take place in three ways. What are they?

_____

_____

_____

2. The sea that John speaks of here is not a sea of water but a sea of _____

3. The beast speaks blasphemies for how long?

_____

4. He that kills with the sword must be?

_____

_____

5. This second beast that comes out of the earth, who is he?

_____

6. For everything that God has, the devil has a

_____

7. What does the false prophet command to be made?

_____

_____

8. The fake prophet will cause everyone to receive a mark. Where are they to receive it?

_____

_____

9. What is the number of the beast, for it is the number of a man? _____

_____

Chapter 14

Revelation 14:1-5

¹ And I looked, and, lo, a Lamb stood on the mount Sion, and with him an hundred forty and four thousand, having his Father's name written in their foreheads.
² And I heard a voice from heaven, as the voice of many waters, and as the voice of a great thunder: and I heard the voice of harpers harping with their harps:
³ And they sung as it were a new song before the throne, and before the four beasts, and the elders: and no man could learn that song but the hundred and forty and four thousand, which were redeemed from the earth.
⁴ These are they which were not defiled with women; for they are virgins. These are they which follow the Lamb whithersoever he goeth. These were redeemed from among men, being the firstfruits unto God and to the Lamb. ⁵ And in their mouth was found no guile: for they are without fault before the throne of God.

As we begin to study this chapter, we're going to find several parenthetical events that will be taking place. Remember, it's important to know that these events are parenthetical, which means they don't take place in the order that they are written. An

159

example would be when reading a story of a hero, and all of a sudden, the book flashes back to his childhood. This is parenthetical, or out of place. John begins by telling us what he sees. Revelation 14:1 tells us, *"And I looked, and, lo, a Lamb stood on the mount Sion, and with him an hundred forty and four thousand, having his Father's name written in their foreheads."* John heard them sing a new song before the throne. **These one hundred forty-four thousand are virgins, according to the Word of God. They follow the Lamb wherever he goes. These are the redeemed from out of the nation of Israel who were sealed unto God.**

Revelation 14:6-7

6 And I saw another angel fly in the midst of heaven, having the everlasting gospel to preach unto them that dwell on the earth, and to every nation, and kindred, and tongue, and people,
7 Saying with a loud voice, Fear God, and give glory to him; for the hour of his judgment is come: and worship him that made heaven, and earth, and the sea, and the fountains of waters.

This is the first of three angels that fly in heaven. This first angel flies close enough to the earth to be seen and heard by mankind. **The angel is preaching the gospel of Jesus Christ, warning the earth that judgment is coming, and that there's still a chance to escape what's going to befall the earth; that the door of mercy is still open, if only they'll repent.** They are called to worship God, to give him praise and glory. This call goes out to the entire earth to every nation and people and tongue.

Revelation 14:8

*And there followed another angel, saying, Babylon is
fallen, is fallen, that great city, because she made all
nations drink of the wine of the wrath of her fornication.*

The second angel flies through the air proclaiming that
"*Babylon is fallen, is fallen, that great city.*" The city of Babylon
first came onto the world scene in the Old Testament. Babylon
represented evil and ungodliness. We know that Babylon is no
longer a city. **What the Bible is calling Babylon is the evil and
vile government of the antichrist, and the way that people are
made to serve and worship the antichrist.** The description of
the fall is found later in chapters 17-18.

Revelation 14:9-11

*[9] And the third angel followed them, saying with a loud
voice, If any man worship the beast and his image, and
receive his mark in his forehead, or in his hand,
[10] The same shall drink of the wine of the wrath of God,
which is poured out without mixture into the cup of his
indignation; and he shall be tormented with fire and
brimstone in the presence of the holy angels, and in the
presence of the Lamb:
[11] And the smoke of their torment ascendeth up for ever
and ever: and they have no rest day nor night, who
worship the beast and his image, and whosoever receiveth
the mark of his name.*

The third angel sounds out the warning. **If any man wor-**

ship the beast and his image, or takes his mark in his forehead or in his hand, there shall no longer be any hope for him as to salvation. He shall be tormented with fire and brimstone; there shall be no rest for them day or night who have the mark of the beast.

Revelation 14:12-13

12 Here is the patience of the saints: here are they that keep the commandments of God, and the faith of Jesus.
13 And I heard a voice from heaven saying unto me, Write, Blessed are the dead which die in the Lord from hence-forth: Yea, saith the Spirit, that they may rest from their labours; and their works do follow them.

John here tells us that there's a time when the saints will go through all kinds of trouble, torture, and finally death. Verse 12 says, *"Here is the patience of the saints, here are they that keep the commandments of God,"* and have kept their faith in Jesus Christ our Lord. **Then a voice said, blessed are the dead which die in the name of the Lord.** Then the spirit tells these saints to rest from their labor.

We think of a time when the saints around the whole world will suffer. As we look at these scriptures, this is happening today. Christians around the world suffer torture, troubles, and even death. In China, churches meet in homes to hear the true word of God. This is against the law; **if discovered, they are thrown into jail, imprisoned or sometimes killed.** In some Muslim countries, **it's against the law to be a Christian.** Christians are quietly killed. In our own country, by our own government, **the right to preach the truth of God's Word is under attack.**

We, as Christians, are already facing troubles, including the possibility of being imprisoned for speaking out against sin. We are called all kinds of names because we stand for the truth. When the churches should be standing together, what do we see? We see them bowing before the will of Satan, changing their doctrine and their beliefs to satisfy man.

Revelation 14:14-16

¹⁴ And I looked, and behold a white cloud, and upon the cloud one sat like unto the Son of man, having on his head a golden crown, and in his hand a sharp sickle.
¹⁵ And another angel came out of the temple, crying with a loud voice to him that sat on the cloud, Thrust in thy sickle, and reap: for the time is come for thee to reap; for the harvest of the earth is ripe.
¹⁶ And he that sat on the cloud thrust in his sickle on the earth; and the earth was reaped.

John now sees a white cloud and one sitting on the cloud whose likeness is as the Son of man, and He is wearing a golden crown. There was a sickle in His hand. The term used here *"like unto the Son of man"* is used many times to represent Jesus Christ. Then another angel comes out of the temple of God crying with a loud voice: *"Thrust in thy sickle, and reap."* We have here another parenthetical example of the rapture of the church (all truly born-again believers who worship God in spirit and in truth).

What percentage of the church world do you think will go in the "catching away" (the rapture)? Remember, the word rapture isn't found in the Bible. Would you say 50%, 75%, 90%? **No one knows but God, but through scripture we can have a fairly**

good idea. There are three different examples of the rapture.

This first example reveals an important truth about the church:

Matthew 25:14-30 – *[14] For the kingdom of heaven is as a man travelling into a far country, who called his own servants, and delivered unto them his goods. [15] And unto one he gave five talents, to another two, and to another one; to every man according to his several ability; and straightway took his journey. [16] Then he that had received the five talents went and traded with the same, and made them other five talents. [17] And likewise he that had received two, he also gained other two. [18] But he that had received one went and digged in the earth, and hid his lord's money. [19] After a long time the lord of those servants cometh, and reckoneth with them. [20] And so he that had received five talents came and brought other five talents, saying, Lord, thou deliveredst unto me five talents: behold, I have gained beside them five talents more. [21] His lord said unto him, Well done, thou good and faithful servant: thou hast been faithful over a few things, I will make thee ruler over many things: enter thou into the joy of thy lord. [22] He also that had received two talents came and said, Lord, thou deliveredst unto me two talents: behold, I have gained two other talents beside them. [23] His lord said unto him, Well done, good and faithful servant; thou hast been faithful over a few things, I will make thee ruler over many things: enter thou into the joy of thy lord. [24] Then he which had received the one talent came and said, Lord, I knew thee that thou art an hard man, reaping* *where thou hast not sown, and gathering where thou hast not strawed: ²⁵ And I was afraid, and went and hid thy talent in the earth: lo, there thou hast that is thine. ²⁶ His lord answered and said unto him, Thou wicked and slothful servant, thou knewest that I reap where I sowed not, and gather where I have not strawed: ²⁷ Thou oughtest therefore to have put my money to the exchangers, and then at my coming I should have received mine own with usury. ²⁸ Take therefore the talent from him, and give it unto him which hath ten talents. ²⁹ For unto every one that hath shall be given, and he shall have abundance: but from him that hath not shall be taken away even that which he hath. ³⁰ And cast ye the unprofitable servant into outer darkness: there shall be weeping and gnashing of teeth.*

In these scriptures, we see the Lord leave His servants with the command to occupy till He returns. The Lord gives each servant the ability to work and furnishes the means to carry on until His return. These three servants are a type of the church. **In this example, we see that a third of the church will miss the rapture when Jesus returns.** A third of the church will be cast into outer darkness where there shall be weeping and gnashing of teeth.

The second example of the rapture is given by Jesus:

Matthew 25:1-13 – *¹ Then shall the kingdom of heaven be likened unto ten virgins, which took their lamps, and went forth to meet the bridegroom. ² And five of them were wise, and five were foolish. ³ They that were foolish took their*

165

lamps, and took no oil with them: ^{4} But the wise took oil in their vessels with their lamps. ^{5} While the bridegroom tarried, they all slumbered and slept. ^{6} And at midnight there was a cry made, Behold, the bridegroom cometh; go ye out to meet him. ^{7} Then all those virgins arose, and trimmed their lamps. ^{8} And the foolish said unto the wise, Give us of your oil; for our lamps are gone out. ^{9} But the wise answered, saying, Not so; lest there be not enough for us and you: but go ye rather to them that sell, and buy for yourselves. ^{10} And while they went to buy, the bridegroom came; and they that were ready went in with him to the marriage: and the door was shut. ^{11} Afterward came also the other virgins, saying, Lord, Lord, open to us. ^{12} But he answered and said, Verily I say unto you, I know you not. ^{13} Watch therefore, for ye know neither the day nor the hour wherein the Son of man cometh.

In the second example, the scriptures gives a perfect example of the church at the time of the rapture. Jesus, let me remind you, is the one giving these examples. *"Then shall the kingdom of heaven be likened unto ten virgins which took their lamps and went forth to meet the bridegroom."*

We must note a few points here that are very important. First, **they were ALL virgins**. The word virgin indicates they were all pure and undefiled. In plain language, they were all saved and washed in the blood of Jesus. Second, **all took their lamps and went forth to meet the bridegroom**. The lamp that each had is a symbol of the light of God that shines forth in the lives of the redeemed of our Lord. So, we see that ALL were saved and ALL were filled with the light of the truth of the gospel. Third, of these ten virgins, Jesus tells us that **five of them were wise and five were foolish**. Jesus tells us that the foolish took their lamps but took no oil with them. We know that for a lamp to shine forth its light, the oil must be refilled continually. When I was young, I remember the old coal oil lamps we used when the electricity would go off in storms and at other times. It was my job to be sure that there was always enough oil in the lamps to give us light in those times. To me, what this example means is that **the foolish virgins did not refill their spiritual lamps by prayer and the reading and studying of God's Holy Word. It's almost impossible to retain that spiritual joy and zeal without a continual walk with God.**

While the bridegroom tarried, the scripture states that they ALL slumbered and slept; which means they became engrossed with the affairs of life, and the foolish virgins let their relationship with God slip. Then the cry went out that the bridegroom was coming, and the virgins arose and trimmed their lamps. When the foolish virgins realized that their lamps had gone out and they had no oil to relight their lamps, they then asked of the five wise virgins, *"give us some of your oil."* The answer was, *"not so lest there be not enough for us. Go to them that sell and buy for yourselves."* In other words, as plain as I can put it, go and do your first works over again. Sadly, **while they went away to buy, the bridegroom came, the wise went into the marriage and the door was shut**. When the foolish virgins returned, they asked to be let into the marriage. The answer they received was; *"verily I know you not."* Then Jesus gives us the warning to **watch, for we know not the day or hour when the Son of Man will come**. In this example, half of the church world will miss the rapture of the church.

The third example of the second coming comes through the ten lepers:

Luke 17:11-19 – *[11] And it came to pass, as he went to Jerusalem, that he passed through the midst of Samaria and Galilee. [12] And as he entered into a certain village, there met him ten men that were lepers, which stood afar off: [13] And they lifted up their voices, and said, Jesus, Master, have mercy on us. [14] And when he saw them, he said unto them, Go shew yourselves unto the priests. And it came to pass, that, as they went, they were cleansed. [15] And one of them, when he saw that he was healed, turned back, and with a loud voice glorified God, [16] And fell down on his face at his feet, giving him thanks: and he was a Samaritan. [17] And Jesus answering said, Were there not ten cleansed? but where are the nine? [18] There are not found that returned to give glory to God, save this stranger. [19] And he said unto him, Arise, go thy way: thy faith hath made thee whole.*

The third example is of the ten lepers. I had never thought about these scriptures referring to the rapture. Then, one day, as I was reading these scriptures, the Lord began to show me how that this is a type of his second coming. **The lepers represent the church; ALL ten came to Jesus for healing.** When we came to Jesus for salvation and Jesus saved us, there was a healing that took place in our souls. These lepers had a need, and they went to the one who could meet their needs. Jesus healed ALL ten and told them to go and show themselves to the priest. As they went, they realized that they were healed. **ALL were healed, but only one returned to give Jesus praise and glory.** The others may never have seen Jesus again. So, I hope that you can see that only ten percent of the church is really where it should be with the Lord. Only ten percent truly worship our Lord and walk with him and serve Him. **These ten percent are the only ones who are ready to go in the rapture.** I again truly believe that at our Lord's return, only about ten percent of the whole church world will be ready. We cannot afford to live by church doctrine; **we must live according to the Word**. Church doctrine changes to accommodate what people want and desire, but the Word is forever the same, for it doesn't change. **Live by the Word; it's our road map, our guide book, and our instruction manual. By following the Word, we can make heaven our home.**

Revelation 14:17-20

[17] And another angel came out of the temple which is in heaven, he also having a sharp sickle.
[18] And another angel came out from the altar, which had power over fire; and cried with a loud cry to him that had the sharp sickle, saying, Thrust in thy sharp sickle, and gather the clusters of the vine of the earth; for her grapes are fully ripe.
[19] And the angel thrust in his sickle into the earth, and gathered the vine of the earth, and cast it into the great winepress of the wrath of God.
[20] And the winepress was trodden without the city, and blood came out of the winepress, even unto the horse bridles, by the space of a thousand and six hundred furlongs.

Then another angel came out of the temple, and he also had a sickle. And another angel came out from the altar saying to the first angel to thrust in his sickle and gather the earth. What we are talking about is the battle of Armageddon, the great and final battle at the end of the thousand-year reign of Christ and his saints. **After this will come the great white throne judgment when all will stand before God, great and small, rich and poor. ALL will be there.**

Chapter 14 Review Questions

1. Where was the Lamb standing? _____

_____

2. Who was with Him? _____

_____

_____

3. What does parenthetical mean?

_____

_____

_____

4. The hundred and forty and four thousand are special because of what? _____

_____

_____

5. The third angel sounds out a warning; what is this warning? _____

_____

6. How many examples of the rapture of the church are given in the four gospels? _____

7. How many virgins where there? _____

8. There are two reapings in this chapter. One in Verses 14-16 and the other in Verses 17-20.

    a. What does the first reaping denote?

    _____

    _____

    _____

    b. What does the second reaping denote?

    _____

    _____

    _____

Chapter 15

Revelation 15:1

And I saw another sign in heaven, great and marvellous,
seven angels having the seven last plagues; for in them is
filled up the wrath of God.

John saw another sign in heaven, seven angels that had the seven last plagues. **Scripture states that these seven plagues are filled with the wrath of God. God's mercy has finally come to an end.** Chapter 14 shows us seven parenthetical events that take place in different parts of Revelation and at different times. But here we are looking at a period of events that must surely take place before the end. As scripture has stated, these plagues are the terrible wrath of God. **So far God has tried to have mercy on the people of the earth, and every attempt has been turned away.** These seven plagues will be poured out, and there will be no mercy, but only God's wrath.

Revelation 15:2-4

[2] And I saw as it were a sea of glass mingled with fire: and
them that had gotten the victory over the beast, and over
his image, and over his mark, and over the number of his

name, stand on the sea of glass, having the harps of God.
³ And they sing the song of Moses the servant of God, and
the song of the Lamb, saying, Great and marvellous are
thy works, Lord God Almighty; just and true are thy ways,
thou King of saints.
⁴ Who shall not fear thee, O Lord, and glorify thy name?
for thou only art holy: for all nations shall come and wor-
ship before thee; for thy judgments are made manifest.

According to Dr. Williams, "The 'sea of glass' of this chapter is the same as that seen by John in Revelation 4. However, now it is no longer empty, but on its crystal pavement appear victorious martyrs. Also the sea is described as 'mingled with fire.' These overcomers will have suffered the fiery persecution of the regime of the beast and will stand on the calm sea, triumphant in the protective nearness to God." **It's believed that these who stand on the sea of glass are the redeemed Jews who refused to bow down before the antichrist,** when he proclaimed himself to be God, in the new temple that was built by the Jews in Jerusalem.

Revelation 15:5-8

⁵ And after that I looked, and, behold, the temple of the
tabernacle of the testimony in heaven was opened:
⁶ And the seven angels came out of the temple, having the
seven plagues, clothed in pure and white linen, and having
their breasts girded with golden girdles.
And one of the four beasts gave unto the seven angels
seven golden vials full of the wrath of God, who liveth for
ever and ever.

⁸ And the temple was filled with smoke from the glory of God, and from his power; and no man was able to enter into the temple, till the seven plagues of the seven angels were fulfilled.

John now looks, and behold, the temple of the tabernacle of the testimony in heaven was opened. And seven angels came out of the temple. Each angel would be given a golden vial which was full of the wrath of God; these vials were to be poured out on the earth. Each angel was dressed in pure white linen with a golden girdle; **the pure white linen symbolizes the rightness of God and the golden girdle the righteousness and faithfulness of God**. After the angels come out of the temple, the temple was filled with smoke from the glory of God, and no man was able to enter into the temple. Not until after the seven plagues were completed on earth would man again be able to enter into the temple. There's some disagreement as to what the meaning of the smoke closing off the temple to man means. But I believe that **not being able to enter the temple is a sign that during this time the doors of mercy are closed; that no man can come before God for salvation because it's too late**. There are some who say that it's never too late to get saved, that God will never turn man away. If we go back to Genesis, we find God gave man only so long to make things right. When Noah entered into the ark, God shut the door; mankind was locked outside and destroyed. **The smoke that closed man off from God is the sign that there's an allotted time for man to ask God for forgiveness and to be born again. When God begins to pour out his wrath on the earth and man, the doors of mercy are closed. It will be impossible for man to be saved.** When Jesus died on the cross, He opened unto man direct access to the throne of God; no longer was man kept apart from God. The veil in the temple was rent in twain. Man could go directly to the throne of grace and ask God for forgiveness and salvation. And so has it been for some two thousand years. **But that day will soon come to an end in the tribulation period, when the wrath of God is poured out on the haters and rejecters of God.**

Chapter 15 Review Questions

1. How many plagues were to be poured out?

_____

2. Those who stand on the crystal sea are believed to be whom?

_____

_____

3. John saw seven angels, and each angel was given what?

_____

_____

4. The smoke filled the temple so that no one could enter. What is the believed reason for this?

_____

_____

_____

_____

_____

5. What happened when Jesus died on the cross and the veil in the temple was rent in twain (torn into two pieces)?

_____

_____

_____

_____

Chapter 16

Revelation 16:1

And I heard a great voice out of the temple saying to the seven angels, Go your ways, and pour out the vials of the wrath of God upon the earth.

As the first verse opens, John hears a voice coming out of the temple. It's a command from God to the seven angels to go and pour out the vials of the wrath of God upon the earth. These last seven plaques (some believe) are to be poured out at the same time as the seven trumpets, one vial per trumpet. *I do not believe this is the case.* I believe that **these plaques will begin around or shortly after the mark of the beast is given out. People will have to make that dreadful decision, yes they will, or no they won't take the mark.**

Revelation 16:2

And the first went, and poured out his vial upon the earth; and there fell a noisome and grievous sore upon the men which had the mark of the beast, and upon them which worshipped his image.

The first vial is poured out upon the earth. Every man, woman, young and old who received the mark of the beast and worshiped his image, there fell upon them grievous sores. **We don't know what kind of disease it will be; some believe it to be boils. It could very well be many different kinds, but their purpose was to torment man, and torment mankind they will.** Just to think of the hurting, the pain and the festering sores; this will be an unbearable time, and this is only the first plaque. There are six more to come.

Revelation 16:3

And the second angel poured out his vial upon the sea; and it became as the blood of a dead man: and every living soul died in the sea.

Looking back to the trumpets, when the second trumpet sounded, one third of the seas became blood. **When the second vial will be poured out, all of the seas will become as the blood of a dead man. And every living thing in the seas will die.** Oh! The stench that will arise.

Revelation 16:4-7

⁴ And the third angel poured out his vial upon the rivers and fountains of waters; and they became blood.
⁵ And I heard the angel of the waters say, Thou art righteous, O Lord, which art, and wast, and shalt be, because thou hast judged thus.
⁶ For they have shed the blood of saints and prophets, and

thou hast given them blood to drink; for they are worthy.
⁷ And I heard another out of the altar say, Even so, Lord
God Almighty, true and righteous are thy judgments.

Now the third angel steps forward and pours out his vial upon the earth, and the waters of the rivers and the fountains of waters become blood. Then John heard the angel of the waters give praise to God saying, *"Thou art righteous, O Lord, which art, and wast, and shalt be, because thou hast judged thus."* The angel went on to say that **they had shed the blood of the saints and prophets, and now the Lord has given them blood to drink. This is a just judgment.** Then another angel spoke out of the altar saying, *"Lord God Almighty, true and righteous are thy judgments."*

Revelation 16:8-9

⁸ And the fourth angel poured out his vial upon the sun;
and power was given unto him to scorch men with fire.
⁹ And men were scorched with great heat, and blasphemed
the name of God, which hath power over these plagues:
and they repented not to give him glory.

The fourth angel now pours out his vial upon the sun. This angel had power given unto him to scorch mankind with fire. **With all the pain and torment that man is going through, you'd think people would cry out to God for forgiveness, but no, instead of calling out to God, they blaspheme or curse God.** Man will not repent.

Revelation 16:10-11

[10] And the fifth angel poured out his vial upon the seat of the beast; and his kingdom was full of darkness; and they gnawed their tongues for pain,
[11] And blasphemed the God of heaven because of their pains and their sores, and repented not of their deeds.

The fifth angel pours out his vial upon the seat of the beast; and his kingdom was full of darkness. This darkness is a literal darkness, much as the darkness that fell upon Egypt in the days of Moses. That darkness lasted three days. How long this darkness will last, scripture doesn't say. **Scripture does say that people gnawed their tongues because of the unbearable pain and their sores. And again they blasphemed God and repented not.** We see this even today when trials hit some people and events take place in their lives, and **instead of asking God for help, they blame God** for letting these things come upon them.

Revelation 16:12

And the sixth angel poured out his vial upon the great river Euphrates; and the water thereof was dried up, that the way of the kings of the east might be prepared.

And the sixth angel poured out his vial upon the river Euphrates, and that great river dried up. The river Euphrates, for thousands of years, has been a barrier against enemy armies. The Euphrates is somewhere around 1,780 miles long. It has been a barrier against enemies, a source of water, and a means of travel to transport goods by boat. **When this river is dried up, it opens** the way for the armies of the east to come up against Jerusalem in the battle of Armageddon.

Revelation 16:13-16

[13] And I saw three unclean spirits like frogs come out of the mouth of the dragon, and out of the mouth of the beast, and out of the mouth of the false prophet.
[14] For they are the spirits of devils, working miracles, which go forth unto the kings of the earth and of the whole world, to gather them to the battle of that great day of God Almighty.
[15] Behold, I come as a thief. Blessed is he that watcheth, and keepeth his garments, lest he walk naked, and they see his shame.
[16] And he gathered them together into a place called in the Hebrew tongue Armageddon.

These four verses are parenthetical, which means that they are not in the correct order or place. John states that he saw three unclean spirits like frogs come out of the mouths of the dragon, the beast and the false prophet, one out of each mouth. Scripture then states that these spirits are of the devil, who is working lying wonders and miracles. They go forth to the kings or leaders of the earth and of the whole world. **Their purpose is to cause the armies of these kingdoms to rise up against Christ and the saints at Jerusalem. This brings about the battle of Armageddon.** The reason that these scriptures are parenthetical is the warning that Jesus gives. The 15th verse states, *"Behold I come as a thief. Blessed is he that watcheth, and keepeth his garments, lest he walk naked, and they see his shame."* This verse is talking about the rapture, which we know has already taken place. **This sixth vial being poured out brings everything into play for the battle of Armageddon.**

Revelation 16:17-21

[17] And the seventh angel poured out his vial into the air; and there came a great voice out of the temple of heaven, from the throne, saying, It is done.
[18] And there were voices, and thunders, and lightnings; and there was a great earthquake, such as was not since men were upon the earth, so mighty an earthquake, and so great.
[19] And the great city was divided into three parts, and the cities of the nations fell: and great Babylon came in remembrance before God, to give unto her the cup of the wine of the fierceness of his wrath.
[20] And every island fled away, and the mountains were not found.
[21] And there fell upon men a great hail out of heaven, every stone about the weight of a talent: and men blasphemed God because of the plague of the hail; for the plague thereof was exceeding great.

The seventh angel comes forward to pour out the last of the vials; this vial is poured out into the air; then came a great voice out of the temple in heaven from the throne saying, *"It is done."* After this, there's thunder and lightning, and a great earthquake such as was not since man was upon the earth. **This earthquake will be the most disastrous earthquake that has ever been. It will affect the whole earth.** Dr. Williams, in *Prevision* *of History,* states, "There will be a great topographical change brought about: when the Mount of Olives cleaves in two, east to west, 'and half of the mountain shall remove toward the north and half of it toward the south.' The city of Jerusalem will be divided into three parts. Along with all that is happening there will rain down hail stones out of heaven upon man and each hail stone will weigh about one hundred and twenty-five pounds, a Jewish talent. In Job 38 (22-23*)* [22] *Hast thou entered into the treasures of the snow? or hast thou seen the treasures of the hail,* [23] *Which I have reserved against the time of trouble, against the day of battle and war?"* **The scripture tells us that men blasphemed and cursed God because of the plaque of the hail, for the plaque of the hail was exceedingly great.**

Chapter 16 Review Questions

1. What was God's command to the seven angels?

_____

_____

_____

2. What happened to man when the first vial was poured out?

_____

_____

_____

3. What happens when the second vial is poured out on the

sea? _____

_____

_____

4. Where does the third angel pour out his vial?

_____

_____

_____

5. Why was this a righteous judgment?

_____

_____

_____

6. What do the three unclean spirits do?

_____

_____

_____

7. What kind of plague will rain down upon man from

heaven? _____

_____

_____

Chapter 17

Before we get into scripture, we need to look at the contrasting visions given to John. Both of these visions are taking place on earth. The first will be in a wilderness (Revelation 17:3). In both of these visions, the symbol used will be of women. **The first woman represents the great harlot; she will represent all the apostate religions and be identified as Babylon. The second woman will represent a bride, the true church of our Lord Jesus Christ.** The bride is identified as a city, New Jerusalem.

Revelation 17:1-7

> *[1] And there came one of the seven angels which had the seven vials, and talked with me, saying unto me, Come hither; I will shew unto thee the judgment of the great whore that sitteth upon many waters:*
> *[2] With whom the kings of the earth have committed fornication, and the inhabitants of the earth have been made drunk with the wine of her fornication.*
> *[3] So he carried me away in the spirit into the wilderness: and I saw a woman sit upon a scarlet coloured beast, full of names of blasphemy, having seven heads and ten horns.*
> *[4] And the woman was arrayed in purple and scarlet*

colour, and decked with gold and precious stones and
pearls, having a golden cup in her hand full of
abominations and filthiness of her fornication:
⁵ And upon her forehead was a name written, MYSTERY,
BABYLON THE GREAT, THE MOTHER OF HARLOTS
AND ABOMINATIONS OF THE EARTH.
⁶ And I saw the woman drunken with the blood of the
saints, and with the blood of the martyrs of Jesus: and
when I saw her, I wondered with great admiration.
⁷ And the angel said unto me, Wherefore didst thou
marvel? I will tell thee the mystery of the woman, and of
the beast that carrieth her, which hath the seven heads
and ten horns.

The judgment of the great harlot is the central theme of these first six verses. One of the angels which poured out the seven vials came to John. The angel then told John to come, and he would show him the judgment of the great whore that sits upon many waters. **Later, in Verse 15, we will read that the many waters symbolizes people, multitudes, nations and tongues. This whore that holds so much power is the apostate religion of the antichrist.** She perverts the truth and leads the rulers and people of the earth into an unholy union, an unholy religious system that aims to rule the whole earth. For John to better visualize this great harlot, he is carried away in the spirit into the wilderness. There John sees a woman sit upon a scarlet-colored beast. The beast is full of names of blasphemy and has seven heads and ten horns. The woman is dressed in clothes that denote royalty, with gold and precious stones of all kinds, and in her hand there's a golden cup which is full of her sins and ungodly acts. Verse 5 tells us that upon her forehead was written a name, "*MYSTERY,*

190

BABYLON THE GREAT, THE MOTHER OF HARLOTS AND ABOMINATIONS OF THE EARTH."

Here we need to look at Babylon and why God calls Babylon the great whore. In Genesis, we first read about Nimrod, who is the son of Cush, who was the son of Ham, who was the son of Noah. Nimrod lead the people to build the tower of Babel, which later became the city of Babylon. **Nimrod's desire was to build a tower which would reach up to heaven. This displeased God, who stopped their work by confounding their language.** The people divided and went their separate ways. But one group stayed at Babel to build the city Babylon and additional nearby cities.

There's some confusion about Nimrod's wife. One belief is that Nimrod married his mother. The more common belief is that Nimrod met and married an inn/brothel keeper in the city of Erech. Nimrod built Babylon as his capital city and home. It wouldn't do to have the great king Nimrod's wife be an ex-harlot. So, **a story was invented that she was a virgin that sprang from the sea, and thus she was considered to be a proper wife for the great king, Nimrod.** Nimrod's wife's name was Semiramis, and she came to power riding Nimrod's coattail. She was cruel and evil. Because of her evil, Nimrod was killed, and she took his place as ruler.

Semiramis was not only queen but also the high priestess of a false religion that would spread throughout the entire world. She was the first to bring in polytheism, the worship of many gods. In Satan's attempt to defeat God's plan for man, Semiramis, through the devil's help, came up with the worship of the queen of heaven. Semiramis had a baby which she said was miraculously conceived, and she called his name Tammuz. Through this lie began the worship of the "mother and child."

Tammuz, it was said, would be great, the promised answer to the world's problems. This religion of the queen of heaven and the worship of the mother and child spread throughout the known world. **The symbols were the same, and while the name of the mother and child may be different, it all began in Babylon.**

The names of the mother and child were known as Venus and Cupid in Rome, and Isis and Horus in Egypt. In Greece, they were Aphrodite and Eros, and in Phoenicia they were Ashtoreth and Tammuz. They were known by other names among other people and tribes and nations. **One last and very sad entry about the queen of heaven holding her child is that this image has been accepted by part of the church world.** The Catholic Church still carries on this idol worship, but now Mary is the queen of heaven. Some of her statues show her wearing a crown upon her head, and others depict her as the mother holding her child. **All of the false religions in the world today had their beginning at Babylon. Now we can understand why God calls Babylon the great whore, the harlot that leads billions of people away from God to everlasting destruction.**

Verse 6 tells us that John saw the woman drunken with the blood of the saints, the blood of martyrs who hold to the testimony of Jesus Christ as Lord and Master, as the only Son of God and our Savior. John states that he wondered who this woman was, and an angel came to him and said, "I will tell thee the mystery of the woman and of the beast."

Revelation 17:8-13

⁸ The beast that thou sawest was, and is not; and shall ascend out of the bottomless pit, and go into perdition: and they that dwell on the earth shall wonder, whose names were not written in the book of life from the foundation of the world, when they behold the beast that was, and is not, and yet is.

⁹ And here is the mind which hath wisdom. The seven heads are seven mountains, on which the woman sitteth.
¹⁰ And there are seven kings: five are fallen, and one is, and the other is not yet come; and when he cometh, he must continue a short space.
¹¹ And the beast that was, and is not, even he is the eighth, and is of the seven, and goeth into perdition.
¹² And the ten horns which thou sawest are ten kings, which have received no kingdom as yet; but receive power as kings one hour with the beast.
¹³ These have one mind, and shall give their power and strength unto the beast.

The beast that thou saw was, and is not, but will rise again, isn't what a lot of people think. **This beast will be a world controlling government.** Already we have a movement in the world today for a "one world government." And there must also be a "one world church" or religious system. Many think this will be the Catholic Church, but this isn't so. But, it may be a form of the Catholic Church, which is spreading around the world. **The church of the antichrist must bring all religions together under the same umbrella.** Muslims will not become Christians, and Christians will not become Muslims. And so on with all religions. There will come to pass some great happening that will cause ALL religions to come together. What this will be, I can't imagine, but it will happen. I would like to bring out a point in this eighth verse that brings confusion to many readers of scripture.

The scripture states: "*and they that dwell on the earth*

shall wonder, whose names were not written in the book of life from the foundation for the world, when they behold the beast." Some people try to use this scripture to say that the saints are still on the earth and have not been raptured. This idea cannot be upheld by scripture. After the rapture of the saints, will there still be saints left on the earth? Yes, but not who you think. The church will be raptured out. The backsliders and students of scripture will realize what's happened and be martyred, the only way left for them to make heaven. So, who's left? The Jews, God's chosen people. **The Jews will come to believe that Jesus is the promised Messiah**, some of them, anyway. We know that there will be 144,000 sealed unto God, twelve thousand out of each tribe. These are called saints. **This 144,000 Jews, or saints, will go all the way through the tribulation period, but the church of Jesus Christ, the saints of God, will be raptured before the wrath of God is poured out.** The wrath of God will be the last three-and-one-half years of the tribulation. The Jews, who for over two thousand years have rejected Jesus as the Messiah, they or some of them will begin to understand and turn to Jesus as the only true Messiah, the only hope they have.

Back to the woman that sat upon the seven hills. We know that the Roman Empire ruled the world for about two thousand years, and it no longer exists. It will be revived again to rule the world, but this time the antichrist will be the one in power.

Revelation 17:14-18

[14] These shall make war with the Lamb, and the Lamb shall overcome them: for he is Lord of lords, and King of kings: and they that are with him are called, and chosen, and faithful.

194

15 And he saith unto me, The waters which thou sawest,
where the whore sitteth, are peoples, and multitudes, and
nations, and tongues.
16 And the ten horns which thou sawest upon the beast,
these shall hate the whore, and shall make her desolate
and naked, and shall eat her flesh, and burn her with fire.
17 For God hath put in their hearts to fulfil his will, and to
agree, and give their kingdom unto the beast, until the
words of God shall be fulfilled.
18 And the woman which thou sawest is that great city,
which reigneth over the kings of the earth.

Verse 13 begins by the antichrist being given power. Verse 14 starts with the antichrist making war upon the Lamb. **The Lamb will defeat his enemies, for He is the Lord of lords and the King of kings, and they that are with Him are called chosen and faithful. What a praise and honor to be called chosen and faithful by our Lord.**

In Verse 15, John is told that the waters thou saw are people and nations; the whore is the evil religious system that was needed to help bring the antichrist to power. But after the antichrist has taken power, he will no longer need his evil church. **This evil religious system will be destroyed; there must not be anything left that might interfere with the plans of the antichrist.**

Chapter 17 Review Questions

1. What will the first woman represent?

_____

_____

2. What was written upon this woman's forehead?

_____

_____

3. As John marveled or wondered about the woman, the angel came to him and said? _____

_____

4. The beast that John saw in Verse 8 is what?

_____

_____

5. In Verse 15 what is John told the waters represent?

_____

_____

_____

6. Who is the whore mentioned in verse 15?

_____

7. What will happen to this whore?

_____

Chapter 18

Revelation 18:1-3

¹ And after these things I saw another angel come down from heaven, having great power; and the earth was lightened with his glory.
² And he cried mightily with a strong voice, saying, Babylon the great is fallen, is fallen, and is become the habitation of devils, and the hold of every foul spirit, and a cage of every unclean and hateful bird.
³ For all nations have drunk of the wine of the wrath of her fornication, and the kings of the earth have committed fornication with her, and the merchants of the earth are waxed rich through the abundance of her delicacies.

John next tells of a great event that takes place. Another angel comes down from heaven having great power and glory and with a great and loud voice. **He announces that Babylon, that great harlot, is fallen. Her power is gone, her greatness is gone, and all that's left is the rubble**; a place of habitation for devils and foul spirits and creatures of the wild.

As we studied in Chapter 17, the woman, the harlot, is the apostate religious system that helps to put the antichrist into power. This spiritual Babylon thought that it could control the anti-christ, but was mistaken. **Once in power, the antichrist no longer needs the Apostate Church and destroys it.**

Chapter 18:1-3 speaks of political Babylon, the future center of commerce, a city that's very wicked in its everyday activities and business. This new Babylon will be like the Babylon of old that God destroyed. This new Babylon will lead nations into fornication or idolatry. **People and nations will go willingly after all that Babylon offers.** The world will be pleasure-mad and worship the creature more than the creator, and for this, judgment will fall.

Revelation 18:4-5

⁴ And I heard another voice from heaven, saying, Come out of her, my people, that ye be not partakers of her sins, and that ye receive not of her plagues
⁵ For her sins have reached unto heaven, and God hath remembered her iniquities.

These two verses are used by some to again try and prove that the saints will go through the tribulation; this isn't the case. **These two verses can have a two-fold meaning: 1. If these two verses are talking about the saved, saints of God, who are born-again believers, then they are parenthetical** and take place at the same time as other happenings in Revelations. **2. These two verses refer to the Jews**, God's chosen people.

The scripture states: *"come out of her my people,"* and throughout the scripture, God calls the Jews "His people." In 2 Chronicles 7:14, he says, *"If my people, which are called by my name, shall humble themselves, and pray, and seek my face, and turn from their wicked ways; then will I hear from heaven, and will forgive their sin, and will heal their land."* **I hold to this second thought that God is speaking to the Jews.** We know, according to scripture, the woman hiding in the wilderness in a place that God has prepared is talking about the Jewish people who come to realize that Jesus is the Messiah. **In the Old Testament, God calls the Jews "my people" two hundred twenty-four times.** We know that in the Old Testament, God isn't speaking to Gentile saints. **In the New Testament, God speaks of "my people" only seven times**, and most of these times he's speaking to the Jews. Note that all the way through the tribulation period, God calls to the Jews.

Revelation 18:6-8

⁶ Reward her even as she rewarded you, and double unto her double according to her works: in the cup which she hath filled fill to her double.
⁷ How much she hath glorified herself, and lived deliciously, so much torment and sorrow give her: for she saith in her heart, I sit a queen, and am no widow, and shall see no sorrow.
⁸ Therefore shall her plagues come in one day, death, and mourning, and famine; and she shall be utterly burned with fire: for strong is the Lord God who judgeth her.

These verses tell us about the kind of judgment that God decrees and that will be poured out upon Babylon. Babylon must be punished. **God cannot withhold punishment, because of the judgment that fell upon Sodom and Gomorrah.** We are worse now than then.

God in His justice declares that Babylon shall receive as her reward double the punishment that she handed out to those who chose not to worship at the altar of sin. She glorified herself; she looked not at the plight of others. This is the same view that the world takes today, the view that I come first, and I have no time or patience with others. **Sadly, this is the same spirit that has crept into our churches; the trend has become to build mega-churches, with pastors who are too busy to tend to the needs of their flock. They know very few of them by name**, but that doesn't matter. They are too important in their own minds to deal with the little people. As long as the money comes in, they care little about others. But, like Babylon, **their day of judgment is coming, and they, like Babylon, will pay and pay and pay**. God is jealous over His people and how they are treated.

Revelation 18:9-19

[9] And the kings of the earth, who have committed fornication and lived deliciously with her, shall bewail her, and lament for her, when they shall see the smoke of her burning,
[10] Standing afar off for the fear of her torment, saying, Alas, alas, that great city Babylon, that mighty city! for in one hour is thy judgment come.
[11] And the merchants of the earth shall weep and mourn over her; for no man buyeth their merchandise any more:
[12] The merchandise of gold, and silver, and precious stones, and of pearls, and fine linen, and purple, and silk, and scarlet, and all thyine wood, and all manner vessels of ivory, and all manner vessels of most precious wood, and of brass, and iron, and marble,

13 And cinnamon, and odours, and ointments, and frankincense, and wine, and oil, and fine flour, and wheat, and beasts, and sheep, and horses, and chariots, and slaves, and souls of men.

14 And the fruits that thy soul lusted after are departed from thee, and all things which were dainty and goodly are departed from thee, and thou shalt find them no more at all.

15 The merchants of these things, which were made rich by her, shall stand afar off for the fear of her torment, weeping and wailing,

16 And saying, Alas, alas, that great city, that was clothed in fine linen, and purple, and scarlet, and decked with gold, and precious stones, and pearls!

17 For in one hour so great riches is come to nought. And every shipmaster, and all the company in ships, and sailors, and as many as trade by sea, stood afar off,

18 And cried when they saw the smoke of her burning, saying, What city is like unto this great city!

19 And they cast dust on their heads, and cried, weeping and wailing, saying, Alas, alas, that great city, wherein were made rich all that had ships in the sea by reason of her costliness! for in one hour is she made desolate.

These verses speak of Babylon, but we must understand that Babylon, although not a world power today, still exists in a spiritual sense. **It exists in two forms, a commercial and an ecclesiastical or religious form.** The religious form is the church of the antichrist, which is the church that's instrumental in putting the antichrist in power, and which the antichrist will destroy after he's in power. The other form of Babylon is the commercial form, where the antichrist promises wealth and riches and power to all who serve him. **The kings and rulers will lament the destruction of the commercial Babylon, which made them rich and powerful.** Where's this spiritual Babylon? It's a city that's built on seven hills. Which city is built on seven hills? Rome, the city that ruled the ancient world was built on seven hills and will be revived to rule one more time under the antichrist.

Revelation 18:20

Rejoice over her, thou heaven, and ye holy apostles and prophets; for God hath avenged you on her.

John tells us in this verse that heaven, the holy apostles, and the prophets are told to rejoice, for **God has avenged their blood** on her. Rejoice, rejoice, ye heavens rejoice. The saints in heaven rejoice, because **their blood has been avenged**; the prophets, the apostles whose blood was shed, for standing for God; the apostles whose blood was shed for the sake of Christ Jesus, **rejoice, for judgment is come**.

In Revelation 6:6-11, we read, *"And I heard a voice in the midst of the four beasts say, A measure of wheat for a penny, and three measures of barley for a penny; and see thou hurt not the oil and the wine. And when he had opened the fourth seal, I heard the voice of the fourth beast say, Come and see. And I looked, and behold a pale horse: and his name that sat on him was Death, and Hell followed with him. And power was given unto them over the fourth part of the earth, to kill with sword, and with hunger, and with death, and with the beasts of the earth. And when he had opened the fifth seal, I saw under the altar the souls of them that were slain for the word of God, and for the testimony which they held: And they cried with a loud voice, saying, How long, O Lord, holy and true, dost thou not judge and avenge our blood on them that dwell on the earth? And white robes were given unto every one of them; and it was said unto them, that they should rest yet for a little season, until their fellowservants also and their brethren, that should be killed as they were, should be fulfilled."* We read about the souls that were under the altar; the souls who died for their testimony in Christ Jesus. They wanted to know how long God would to wait before bringing judgment. They were told to rest for a little season, that there were still a few more who were to die as they had died. In this eighteenth chapter, **the time of waiting has come to an end**. Judgment has fallen; **vengeance is mine, sayeth the Lord; I will repay**. God is not slack concerning his promises; only believe.

Revelation 18:21-24

[21] And a mighty angel took up a stone like a great millstone, and cast it into the sea, saying, Thus with violence shall that great city Babylon be thrown down, and shall be found no more at all.
[22] And the voice of harpers, and musicians, and of pipers, and trumpeters, shall be heard no more at all in thee; and no craftsman, of whatsoever craft he be, shall be found any more in thee; and the sound of a millstone shall be heard no more at all in thee;
[23] And the light of a candle shall shine no more at all in thee; and the voice of the bridegroom and of the bride shall be heard no more at all in thee: for thy merchants were the great men of the earth; for by thy sorceries were all nations deceived.

²⁴ And in her was found the blood of prophets, and of
saints, and of all that were slain upon the earth.

These verses give us an example or symbolic picture of an angel casting a great millstone into the sea. **This symbol is a picture of total destruction.** God's Word is always true; his prophecies are always fulfilled.

The millstone shows the suddenness of God's destruction, the violent overthrow that God can bring at any time. Watch as you throw a large rock in the water; the rock hits and causes a wave of water to rise. As the rock sinks under the water, the water closes in around and over the rock, and it's completely gone. That's the way it will be with Babylon. One minute it's there, people are doing everyday things and communication is going out to the entire world. Suddenly it stops, there's no communication, there are no people and there's no city. Judgment has come. **It's the same in our Christian lives. We do our everyday things: working, resting and visiting; then suddenly, we're gone. Jesus has come and caught us away to be with him.**

Isaiah 13:19-22

> *¹⁹ And Babylon, the glory of kingdoms, the beauty of the Chaldees' excellency, shall be as when God overthrew Sodom and Gomorrah.*
> *²⁰ It shall never be inhabited, neither shall it be dwelt in from generation to generation: neither shall the Arabian pitch tent there; neither shall the shepherds make their fold there.*
> *²¹ But wild beasts of the desert shall lie there; and their houses shall be full of doleful creatures; and owls shall*

dwell there, and satyrs shall dance there.

²² And the wild beasts of the islands shall cry in their deso-late houses, and dragons in their pleasant palaces: and her time is near to come, and her days shall not be pro-longed.

Jeremiah 51:24-26

²⁴ And I will render unto Babylon and to all the inhabitants of Chaldea all their evil that they have done in Zion in your sight, saith the LORD.

²⁵ Behold, I am against thee, O destroying mountain, saith the LORD, which destroyest all the earth: and I will stretch out mine hand upon thee, and roll thee down from the rocks, and will make thee a burnt mountain.

²⁶ And they shall not take of thee a stone for a corner, nor a stone for foundations; but thou shalt be desolate for ev-er, saith the LORD.

There are many Bible scholars who have disagreed over the Babylon in the eighteenth chapter of Revelation. Some schol-ars such as Riggs, Scott, and Dake, to name a few of them, be-lieve that Babylon will be rebuilt on the same site where she once stood. Others don't agree, because **they believe that the prophe-cies of Isaiah and Jeremiah are the truth, which states that ancient Babylon will never be rebuilt**. This I also believe, but I also believe that spiritual Babylon is alive and well and waiting for the antichrist. Babylonianism has been in every age, but the scripture talks about the death of prophets and saints. No other city has been more responsible for the deaths of the prophets and saints than imperial Rome, which ruled the entire ancient world, and Papal Rome, which killed every believer that they could find who didn't agree with them. **Both commercial Babylon and spiritual Babylon were the destroyers of the saints of God.**

It is my wish that every born-again believer read the book, *Fox's Book of Martyrs*. It will open your eyes to the truth of how many saints died for their beliefs.

Chapter 18 Review Questions

1. When God's voice speaks out of heaven saying, "Come out of her, my people," to whom is he speaking?

_____

_____

2. How many times in the Old Testament does God call the Jews "my people"?

_____

3. What city today is built upon seven hills?

_____

4. In Verse 20, why does God tell the heaven and the apostles and prophets to rejoice?

_____

_____

5. No other city, or their rulers, have been more involved in the death of the prophets, apostles and saints than spiritual Babylon. Which city is this? _____

Chapter 19

Revelation 19:1-6

¹ And after these things I heard a great voice of much people in heaven, saying, Alleluia; Salvation, and glory, and honour, and power, unto the Lord our God:
² For true and righteous are his judgments: for he hath judged the great whore, which did corrupt the earth with her fornication, and hath avenged the blood of his servants at her hand.
³ And again they said, Alleluia. And her smoke rose up for ever and ever.
⁴ And the four and twenty elders and the four beasts fell down and worshipped God that sat on the throne, saying, Amen; Alleluia.
⁵ And a voice came out of the throne, saying, Praise our God, all ye his servants, and ye that fear him, both small and great.
⁶ And I heard as it were the voice of a great multitude, and as the voice of many waters, and as the voice of mighty thunderings, saying, Alleluia: for the Lord God omnipotent reigneth.

This chapter is full of parenthetical scenes that take place in heaven before the second coming of Christ. **The second coming isn't the rapture of the church; it's when Jesus Christ comes and sets His feet on the earth.** In the rapture of the church, Jesus, our Lord, appears in the air but doesn't set His feet upon the earth. The born-again believers rise to meet Him in the air, and so shall they ever be with the Lord. John begins by saying that he heard a great voice of many people praising God and giving him glory and honor. These voices cried, "Alleluia to the Lord." The twenty-four elders and the four beasts fell down and worshipped God that sat upon the throne saying, "Alleluia." **A great voice came out of the throne saying, "Praise the Lord all ye his servants."** Then John states that he heard the voice of a great multitude praising God.

Revelation 19:7-10

7 Let us be glad and rejoice, and give honour to him: for the marriage of the Lamb is come, and his wife hath made herself ready.

8 And to her was granted that she should be arrayed in fine linen, clean and white: for the fine linen is the righteousness of saints.

9 And he saith unto me, Write, Blessed are they which are called unto the marriage supper of the Lamb. And he saith unto me, These are the true sayings of God.

10 And I fell at his feet to worship him. And he said unto me, See thou do it not: I am thy fellowservant, and of thy brethren that have the testimony of Jesus: worship God: for the testimony of Jesus is the spirit of prophecy.

These scriptures tell us of the event we're looking for, and that's the marriage of the Lamb. **Scripture says for us to be glad and rejoice and give honor to Him. The marriage of the Lamb is come, and His wife hath made herself ready. We are the bride, if our hearts were right with God when we died.** There's a good bit of controversy over who the saints are. The bride (wife) will be arrayed in fine linen, clean and white. The fine linen is the righteousness of the saints. John was told to write, *"Blessed are they which are called unto the marriage supper of the Lamb."* But, who are the saints or bride spoken of here? **John Phillips and Dr. Williams, in their commentaries, believe that the bride of Christ is all of those who have been saved or born again, from the death of Christ on the cross, to the rapture.** They are the church, and the church is the bride, blood-bought and redeemed.

Ephesians 5:25-32

25 Husbands, love your wives, even as Christ also loved the church, and gave himself for it;
26 That he might sanctify and cleanse it with the washing of water by the word,
27 That he might present it to himself a glorious church, not having spot, or wrinkle, or any such thing; but that it should be holy and without blemish.
28 So ought men to love their wives as their own bodies. He that loveth his wife loveth himself.
29 For no man ever yet hated his own flesh; but nourisheth and cherisheth it, even as the Lord the church:
30 For we are members of his body, of his flesh, and of his bones.
31 For this cause shall a man leave his father and mother,

*and shall be joined unto his wife, and they two shall be
one flesh.*

*³² This is a great mystery: but I speak concerning Christ
and the church.*

Israel is the earthly wife of Jehovah, now divorced, but
during the Millennium, she will be Jehovah's restored wife.
**These scriptures in Revelation don't apply to Israel, but to the
church, Christ's bride.** The following scriptures refer to Israel as
the divorced wife of God.

Jeremiah 3:14-20

*¹⁴ Turn, O backsliding children, saith the LORD; for I am
married unto you: and I will take you one of a city, and
two of a family, and I will bring you to Zion:*

*¹⁵ And I will give you pastors according to mine heart,
which shall feed you with knowledge and understanding.*

*¹⁶ And it shall come to pass, when ye be multiplied and in-
creased in the land, in those days, saith the LORD, they
shall say no more, The ark of the covenant of the LORD:
neither shall it come to mind: neither shall they remember
it; neither shall they visit it; neither shall that be done any
more.*

*¹⁷ At that time they shall call Jerusalem the throne of the
LORD; and all the nations shall be gathered unto it, to the
name of the LORD, to Jerusalem: neither shall they walk
any more after the imagination of their evil heart.*

*¹⁸ In those days the house of Judah shall walk with the
house of Israel, and they shall come together out of the
land of the north to the land that I have given for an inher-*

itance unto your fathers.

19 But I said, How shall I put thee among the children, and give thee a pleasant land, a goodly heritage of the hosts of nations? and I said, Thou shalt call me, My father; and shalt not turn away from me.

20 Surely as a wife treacherously departeth from her husband, so have ye dealt treacherously with me, O house of Israel, saith the LORD.

Hosea 2:1-23

1 Say ye unto your brethren, Ammi; and to your sisters, Ruhamah.

2 Plead with your mother, plead: for she is not my wife, neither am I her husband: let her herefore put away her whoredoms out of her sight, and her adulteries from between her breasts;

3 Lest I strip her naked, and set her as in the day that she was born, and make her as a wilderness, and set her like a dry land, and slay her with thirst.

4 And I will not have mercy upon her children; for they be the children of whoredoms.

5 For their mother hath played the harlot: she that conceived them hath done shamefully: for she said, I will go after my lovers, that give me my bread and my water, my wool and my flax, mine oil and my drink.

6 Therefore, behold, I will hedge up thy way with thorns, and make a wall, that she shall not find her paths.

7 And she shall follow after her lovers, but she shall not overtake them; and she shall seek them, but shall not find them: then shall she say, I will go and return to my first husband; for then was it better with me than now.

⁸ For she did not know that I gave her corn, and wine, and oil, and multiplied her silver and gold, which they prepared for Baal.

⁹ Therefore will I return, and take away my corn in the time thereof, and my wine in the season thereof, and will recover my wool and my flax given to cover her nakedness.

¹⁰ And now will I discover her lewdness in the sight of her lovers, and none shall deliver her out of mine hand.

¹¹ I will also cause all her mirth to cease, her feast days, her new moons, and her sabbaths, and all her solemn feasts.

¹² And I will destroy her vines and her fig trees, whereof she hath said, These are my rewards that my lovers have given me: and I will make them a forest, and the beasts of the field shall eat them.

¹³ And I will visit upon her the days of Baalim, wherein she burned incense to them, and she decked herself with her earrings and her jewels, and she went after her lovers, and forgat me, saith the LORD.

¹⁴ Therefore, behold, I will allure her, and bring her into the wilderness, and speak comfortably unto her.

¹⁵ And I will give her her vineyards from thence, and the valley of Achor for a door of hope: and she shall sing there, as in the days of her youth, and as in the day when she came up out of the land of Egypt.

¹⁶ And it shall be at that day, saith the LORD, that thou shalt call me Ishi; and shalt call me no more Baali.

¹⁷ For I will take away the names of Baalim out of her mouth, and they shall no more be remembered by their name.

18 And in that day will I make a covenant for them with the beasts of the field, and with the fowls of heaven, and with the creeping things of the ground: and I will break the bow and the sword and the battle out of the earth, and will make them to lie down safely.

19 And I will betroth thee unto me for ever; yea, I will betroth thee unto me in righteousness, and in judgment, and in lovingkindness, and in mercies.

20 I will even betroth thee unto me in faithfulness: and thou shalt know the LORD.

21 And it shall come to pass in that day, I will hear, saith the LORD, I will hear the heavens, and they shall hear the earth;

22 And the earth shall hear the corn, and the wine, and the oil; and they shall hear Jezreel.

23 And I will sow her unto me in the earth; and I will have mercy upon her that had not obtained mercy; and I will say to them which were not my people, Thou art my people; and they shall say, Thou art my God.

I had forgotten that God called Israel his wife, until doing this research for Revelation. In the history of time concerning Israel, Israel would serve God, but **in times of plenty, Israel would drift away from God and backslide**. God would then bring judgment upon them, and they would repent and come back to God. This happened over and over again. **In an attempt to restore Israel, God sent His only Son to the people that He called His and which are called by His name.** Israel refused God's Son, Jesus, and killed Him. Israel still, to this day, doesn't accept Jesus as the Messiah. They are still divorced from God.

The story of Israel is the story of today's church. In one of the letters to the churches, Jesus states that they had left their first love. **This is what's going on in the church of today. They accept the parts they like in God's Word and reject the parts that they don't like.**

2 Corinthians 11:2

> *For I am jealous over you with godly jealousy: for I have espoused you to one husband, that I may present you as a chaste virgin to Christ.*

The church will be presented as a chaste virgin to Christ. This marriage will be the public joining of Christ to his church or bride. Ephesians 5:30-32 tells us, *"For we are members of his body, of his flesh, and of his bones. For this cause shall a man leave his father and mother, and shall be joined unto his wife, and they two shall be one flesh. This is a great mystery: but I speak concerning Christ and the church."* **Before the marriage of the bride to Christ, the saints will have already been judged before the judgment seat of Christ and received their rewards.** Romans 14:10-12 says, *"But why dost thou judge thy brother? or why dost thou set at nought thy brother? for we shall all stand before the judgment seat of Christ. For it is written, As I live, saith the Lord, every knee shall bow to me, and every tongue shall confess to God. So then every one of us shall give account of himself to God."*

We read in Verse 9, *"Blessed are they which are called unto the marriage supper of the Lamb,"* so who are these called guests? **One, we know that the saints, the redeemed and born again make up the raptured church. This church is the bride**

of Christ. What separates the bride from the Old Testament saints? **The New Testament saints are saved through repentance by grace, having the blood of Christ Jesus washing away their sins.** This salvation, through the blood of Jesus, brings us into direct fellowship with God. The scripture, in Romans 8:16-17, states, *"The Spirit itself beareth witness with our spirit, that we are the children of God: And if children, then heirs; heirs of God, and joint-heirs with Christ; if so be that we suffer with him, that we may be also glorified together."* Our salvation comes directly through Jesus Christ, who gave himself to be the final sacrifice once and for all to bring mankind back to God.

So, to whom does the scripture apply, who are the called the invited guest, the blessed? It's believed that the called, **these special guests, will be the Old Testament saints and the tribulation martyrs**. The Old Testament saints are those who, by faith in God, trusted God for salvation. Note that in their day, the Holy Ghost hadn't come; there was no born-again experience. The coming of Christ for most was thousands of years to hundreds of years in the future. Their only hope was their faith and trust in God. The tribulation martyrs are in the same condition. The Holy Ghost leaves this world with the raptured church. Their only hope is their faith in God and Jesus Christ. **They will not have salvation granted to them unless they give their lives as their testimony of faith in God and His beloved son, Jesus Christ.** This sacrifice of their lives will gain them entrance to the kingdom of God. There's no other way. So these are the blessed, the called, and the invited guests. As far as anyone knows, the angels won't be guests; they will be spectators and servants at the marriage supper.

In this tenth verse, John falls at the feet of his guide. The guide tells John not to worship him, because he's a fellow servant.

He's one of the brethren that have the testimony of Jesus Christ. **What does he mean by this statement? He's saying that he also is one of those who are saved by the blood of Jesus.** Beloved, our hope for all is to go in the rapture. That old song comes to mind: "I will meet you in the rapture." Church, we dare not, we cannot afford to miss the rapture of the church.

Revelation 19:11-16

[11] And I saw heaven opened, and behold a white horse; and he that sat upon him was called Faithful and True, and in righteousness he doth judge and make war.
[12] His eyes were as a flame of fire, and on his head were many crowns; and he had a name written, that no man knew, but he himself.
[13] And he was clothed with a vesture dipped in blood: and his name is called The Word of God.
[14] And the armies which were in heaven followed him upon white horses, clothed in fine linen, white and clean.
[15] And out of his mouth goeth a sharp sword, that with it he should smite the nations: and he shall rule them with a rod of iron: and he treadeth the winepress of the fierceness and wrath of Almighty God.
[16] And he hath on his vesture and on his thigh a name written, KING OF KINGS, AND LORD OF LORDS.

John is the witness to our Lord's return, "*and behold a white horse and he that sat upon him was called Faithful and True.*" **This rider is our Lord Jesus who is returning to the earth to do judgment and to make war on the inhabitants.** He is crowned with many crowns. He has a name written which no man knows save He, Himself. In Verse 13, we read that His name is called the Word of God.

Christ in His returning will be at the head of the armies which are in heaven. Scripture states these armies will follow him, and they will be riding upon white horses. They will be clothed in fine linen, white and clean. **The fine linen, white and clean, denotes the righteousness of God's saints.** Christ will come leading His armies, and *"out of his mouth goeth a sharp sword,"* and with it He shall smite the nations. The sword is the Word of God which brings judgment. The last part of Verse 15 speaks of Jesus treading the winepress of the fierceness and wrath of God. Revelation 19:16 says, *"And he hath on his vesture and on his thigh a name written, KING OF KINGS, AND LORD OF LORDS."* In the book of Jude, Verse 14, Jude repeats Enoch's prophesy: *"Behold, the Lord cometh with ten thousands of his saints."* Matthew 25:31 tells us, *"When the Son of man shall come in his glory, and all the holy angels with him, then shall he sit upon the throne of his glory:"* **This is where Jesus is telling us of His coming in glory, and that He will sit upon the throne of His glory.**

Revelation 19:17-18

17 And I saw an angel standing in the sun; and he cried with a loud voice, saying to all the fowls that fly in the midst of heaven, Come and gather yourselves together unto the supper of the great God;
18 That ye may eat the flesh of kings, and the flesh of captains, and the flesh of mighty men, and the flesh of horses, and of them that sit on them, and the flesh of all men, both free and bond, both small and great.

In these two verses, we read that an angel cried out with a loud voice. He called to all of the fowls that fly in the midst of heaven. **They are called to come and gather themselves together for what is called the supper of the great God. These birds will eat the flesh of all the dead, those who died in battle, fighting against our Lord and Savior.**

Revelation 19:19-21

[19] And I saw the beast, and the kings of the earth, and their armies, gathered together to make war against him that sat on the horse, and against his army.
[20] And the beast was taken, and with him the false prophet that wrought miracles before him, with which he deceived them that had received the mark of the beast, and them that worshipped his image. These both were cast alive into a lake of fire burning with brimstone.
[21] And the remnant were slain with the sword of him that sat upon the horse, which sword proceeded out of his mouth: and all the fowls were filled with their flesh.

In Verse 19, John tells us that he saw the beast, and the kings and all their armies come together to make war against Christ and his army. Verse 20 states that after the battle was fought, the beast was captured, and the false prophet was also taken. **This false prophet was responsible for much of man being deceived. This false prophet wrought miracles before the beast; these miracles caused multitudes to believe the lie, to take the mark of the beast and to worship his image.** Both the beast and the false prophet were cast alive into a lake of fire burning with brimstone. The last verse tells us of what happened to the

222

remnant, those that were taken alive. "*And the remnant were slain with the sword of him that sat upon the horse, which sword proceeded out of his mouth.*" And to show the vast loss of life in this battle, the chapter ends with, "*and all the fowls were filled with their flesh.*"

Chapter 19 Review Questions

1. What is the second coming?

_____

_____

2. Who makes up the bride?

_____

_____

3. Who is the wife of God?

_____

_____

4. Where will the saints be judged?

_____

_____

5. Who are the "called guests" at the marriage supper?

_____

_____

_____

6. What name is written upon His vesture and thigh?

_____

_____

7. After the battle of Armageddon, what is the fate of those captured alive?

_____

_____

_____

8. Verse 21 closes with what words?

_____

_____

_____

Chapter 20

Revelation 20:1-3

¹ And I saw an angel come down from heaven, having the key of the bottomless pit and a great chain in his hand.
² And he laid hold on the dragon, that old serpent, which is the Devil, and Satan, and bound him a thousand years,
³ And cast him into the bottomless pit, and shut him up, and set a seal upon him, that he should deceive the nations no more, till the thousand years should be fulfilled: and after that he must be loosed a little season.

We see in these scriptures the fulfillment of a very, very long-awaited promise. **The devil, our arch enemy, will finally be bound. From the time of Adam and Eve, the devil has sought to destroy man's faith in God, and at times has almost been successful.** But like scripture proclaims, God has always had a remnant who serve him. At one time, it was down to only eight souls, but where there's a few, there God is with them. John states: *"And I saw an angel come down from heaven."* Who was this angel? The scholar Seiss believes that this angel was Jesus Christ, for we know that Jesus took the keys of hell and death. But the scripture doesn't say that the angel was Christ. We know that as Jesus said, He has given us power over all the forces of the enemy. **I believe that this angel was also given power over the devil.** The keys that the angel carried were to the bottomless pit. The angel also carried a great chain in his hand. The word reveals that the angel laid hold on the devil and bound him with the chain for a thousand years. **Satan was then cast into the bottomless pit, and there he was shut up with a seal placed upon the door to the bottomless pit where he will be kept, so that he could not and will not deceive the nations for one thousand years. At the end of that thousand years, Satan will again be loosed for a little season.**

Here we need to note that this bottomless pit is a different place, separate from the lake of fire where the beast and false prophet were cast (Revelation 19:20). Also, this is the only chapter in the Bible where it tells how long Satan will be bound in the bottomless pit. It's repeated six times in the twentieth chapter. **These thousand years will be the millennial reign of Christ upon this earth. At the end of this thousand-year period, Satan will be set loose upon the nations of the world.**

At this point we need to look at who the people are that Satan will be loosed upon. **It's my firm belief that these people are the people who lived through the tribulation, those who didn't die but still have the mark of the beast are still sealed unto the beast.** Christ and his saints will rule over these people around the world for a thousand years of peace with no death. I asked a minister friend if he believed that children would be born during this time. His answer to me was, "Oh, yes; there will be a lot of children born." The Bible doesn't say one way or another, but my personal belief is that there will be no children born during this time. Those who live through the tribulation still have the mark of the beast. The church has been raptured, and Christ and his saints have returned to the earth to rule and reign. There will be no death, sickness, pain or sorrow. How can innocents be born back into the world? Christ isn't going back to the cross again, for that has already been completed.

Revelation 20:4-6

⁴ And I saw thrones, and they sat upon them, and judgment was given unto them: and I saw the souls of them that were beheaded for the witness of Jesus, and for the word of God, and which had not worshipped the beast, neither his image, neither had received his mark upon their foreheads, or in their hands; and they lived and reigned with Christ a thousand years.
⁵ But the rest of the dead lived not again until the thousand years were finished. This is the first resurrection.
⁶ Blessed and holy is he that hath part in the first resurrection: on such the second death hath no power, but they shall be priests of God and of Christ, and shall reign with him a thousand years.

In the fourth verse, John tells us that he saw thrones and those who would sit upon them. There was power of judgment given to them. How many thrones there were, we don't know. Who's to sit on these thrones, we don't know. **We'll be given our place in heaven according to our abilities.** But to me, my reward will be to just make it in. My desire is just to be where the Lord wants me. John also speaks of seeing those who were beheaded for the "*witness of Jesus, and for the word of God.*" These servants, the scripture states, "*did not worship the beast nor take his mark.*" **It was given unto them, that they lived and reigned with Christ a thousand years. This is the first resurrection.**

But the rest of the dead lived not again until the thousand years' reign was finished. **The first resurrection is the resurrection of all who have died (in the faith) and all who have put their trust and hope in God. This covers all the Old Testament saints, all the New Testament saints (the bride of Christ) and all tribulation saints who died trusting in God and putting their faith in God.** We know this because scripture leaves no doubt that they will be there to reign with Christ. There are some who teach that there will be a general resurrection of the dead, that all the dead will be raised at one time. But as we can see in scripture, this won't be so. The righteous will rule and reign with Christ. At the end of the thousand years, after the great battle when sin is finally put down and death is destroyed, then and only then will the second resurrection take place. In this resurrection, **all of mankind who were sinners and evil doers will be resurrected to face eternal damnation before God**. Verse 6 tells us that blessed and holy are they that have part in the first resurrection, for on such, the second death has no power. We must make our election and calling sure, we must be ready and our soul must return to the grave to be resurrected in a glorified body to be with Christ, which is the first resurrection.

Revelation 20:7-9

⁷ And when the thousand years are expired, Satan shall be loosed out of his prison,
⁸ And shall go out to deceive the nations which are in the four quarters of the earth, Gog and Magog, to gather them together to battle: the number of whom is as the sand of the sea.
⁹ And they went up on the breadth of the earth, and

compassed the camp of the saints about, and the beloved
city: and fire came down from God out of heaven, and
devoured them.

At the end of the millennial reign, a thousand years of perfect peace, Satan will be loosed out of his prison. The third verse of this chapter tells us that it will be for a little season, or a short time. We don't know how long this will be, but it will be long enough for Satan to go out and deceive the nations around the earth to gather them together in battle against Christ and His saints at Jerusalem. Again, **who is Satan loosed upon? He is loosed upon those people who have the mark of the beast, people who didn't die but lived through the tribulation, those whom Christ and his saints have ruled over for the last thousand years.** Scripture doesn't say there will be any death during the millennial reign; neither does it say there won't be. I believe the same people are alive throughout the entire thousand years, and I don't believe there will be any children born during this time. Most commentaries don't say anything on the subject (John Phillips in *Exploring Revelation* says there will be a lot of children born.), so it's up to you to make up your mind the way God leads you.

After having deceived the nations of the earth, Satan will lead them to do battle with Christ and the saints. The enemy will compass or surround the camp of the saints and the holy city (Jerusalem). **Then God will rain down fire upon the armies of Satan, and they will all be destroyed, or as scripture states, devoured.**

Revelation 20:10

And the devil that deceived them was cast into the lake of fire and brimstone, where the beast and the false prophet are, and shall be tormented day and night for ever and ever.

After this battle, Satan will be taken, and he will be cast into the lake of fire and brimstone, where the beast and the false prophet are, and there they shall be tormented day and night, forever and ever. **For as long as God exists, hell and they that are in it shall exist.**

Beware, for there are those who believe that the English Bible was translated wrong, which is a lie. They contend that if the Bible was translated correctly, we would see that Satan and his angels and all condemned unbelievers will not be punished for eternity, and that their punishment will be only for a season. They will be released having paid their debt for their wrongdoing. Then there are some that say that if there really is a hell and a lake of fire, that those who go there will simply burn up and cease to exist. **Reputable Greek scholars affirm that our translation is correct, that there is a lake of fire, and it will exist forever and ever.** Satan must surely be happy with those who seek to pervert the Word of God and knowingly lead men and women astray.

The Word of God today is being twisted so that the true meaning of scripture is hidden from those who want to serve God. Just look at how many translations of the Bible there are. Compare them, and you will find that some of them are nowhere near the truth. **If you want the truth, go to the original Hebrew and Greek, or go to the King James Version, which has been used for four hundred years.**

Origen de Principiis, Book 2, Chapter 5, gives us another look at a false belief, from a man named Origen, a restorationist who lived from 185 to 254 A.D. He believed that sinners would be given an opportunity after death to repent and be saved, and that these souls would repent, now knowing what they did not before. He used Psalm 78:34 to support his errant belief.

There's a desire in man to always be right, even if he must wrongly interpret God's Word to make himself right. It's so important for us to remember that scripture must interpret scripture. **We cannot take scripture out of context if we want to know the truth of God's Word.** (2 Peter 1:20 – *Knowing this first, that no prophecy of the scripture is of any private interpretation.*) We must study the scripture to know the Word of God. False teachings will send a "well-meaning" person into the pits of hell. Always check up on what you're being taught; don't take man's word for anything, not even the pastor, the teacher or a good friend, without checking it with scripture.

Revelation 20:11-15

[11] And I saw a great white throne, and him that sat on it, from whose face the earth and the heaven fled away; and there was found no place for them.
[12] And I saw the dead, small and great, stand before God; and the books were opened: and another book was opened, which is the book of life: and the dead were judged out of those things which were written in the books, according to their works.
[13] And the sea gave up the dead which were in it; and death and hell delivered up the dead which were in them: and they were judged every man according to their works.
[14] And death and hell were cast into the lake of fire. This is the second death.
[15] And whosoever was not found written in the book of life

was cast into the lake of fire.

As John tells us what he's seeing, he begins by saying, *"I saw a great white throne and Him that sat on it."* This scene is not the same scene we see in Revelation, Chapter 4. In Chapter 4 we see the throne of God with the rainbow which portrays the fulfillment of God's promises or covenant to man. In this scene, we see the great white throne; this throne is the final judgment throne where the sinners will receive their final judgment. This throne shows the greatness and power of Almighty God. Think of all the people that will be there. To quote John Phillips, "There is a terrible fellowship there. The dead, small and great, stand before God. Little men and paltry women whose lives were filled with pettiness, selfishness, and nasty little sins will be there. Those whose lives amounted to nothing will be there, whose very sins were drab and dowdy, mean, spiteful, peevish, groveling, vulgar, common, and cheap. The great will be there, men who sinned with a high hand, with dash, and courage and flair. Men like Alexander and Napoleon, Hitler and Stalin will be present, men who went in for wickedness on a grand scale with the world as their stage and who died unrepentant at last." All these will be there to stand before the God that they rejected and would not believe in. They denied him, cursed him and took his name in vain.

Romans 1:21-32

> *21 Because that, when they knew God, they glorified him not as God, neither were thankful; but became vain in their imaginations, and their foolish heart was darkened.*
> *22 Professing themselves to be wise, they became fools,*
> *23 And changed the glory of the uncorruptible God into an*

image made like to corruptible man, and to birds, and fourfooted beasts, and creeping things.

24 Wherefore God also gave them up to uncleanness through the lusts of their own hearts, to dishonour their own bodies between themselves:

25 Who changed the truth of God into a lie, and worshipped and served the creature more than the Creator, who is blessed for ever. Amen.

26 For this cause God gave them up unto vile affections: for even their women did change the natural use into that which is against nature:

27 And likewise also the men, leaving the natural use of the woman, burned in their lust one toward another; men with men working that which is unseemly, and receiving in themselves that recompence of their error which was meet.

28 And even as they did not like to retain God in their knowledge, God gave them over to a reprobate mind, to do those things which are not convenient;

29 Being filled with all unrighteousness, fornication, wickedness, covetousness, maliciousness; full of envy, murder, debate, deceit, malignity; whisperers,

30 Backbiters, haters of God, despiteful, proud, boasters, inventors of evil things, disobedient to parents,

31 Without understanding, covenantbreakers, without natural affection, implacable, unmerciful:

32 Who knowing the judgment of God, that they which commit such things are worthy of death, not only do the same, but have pleasure in them that do them.

Now they stand before the one true God, the God who is to judge them, to pass the final sentence. **It behooves us to make** our election and calling sure, to be in the first resurrection, **not in this the second resurrection.** John states: "*And I saw the dead small and great stand before God; and the books were opened; and another book was opened; which is the book of life.*" As we read God's Word, we know that those who stand before the great white throne for judgment are sinners, lost souls, undone without God or his Son. So then why is the book of life opened with the record books of sin? God is a just God. As souls stand, and the record of their life is read to them, to show true judgment to each soul, **God has opened the book of life to prove that their names aren't there, and that they truly deserve the punishment being given to each one of them.** For they receive punishment according to their works or evil doings. As each soul is cast into the lake of fire, the scripture declares this to be the second death.

Verse 15 reads thus, "*And whosoever was not found written in the book of life was cast into the lake of fire.*" This is the second death, to be forever separated from God and His Son. **The scriptures ask us a question; what will a man give in exchange for his soul? If you aren't saved, what are you receiving in exchange for your soul?**

In closing this chapter, again I quote John Phillips: "The terrible words are spoken: 'Depart from me, ye cursed, into everlasting fire, prepared for the devil and his angels:' Matt. 25:41. It was to save men from this that Christ came and suffered, bled, and died. It stood to warn men of this that God wrote the Bible and for centuries has striven by His Spirit with men. The Bible leaves it at that." What else can we say or do? **We must pray, pray, pray for the lost before it's too late.**

Chapter 20 Review Questions

1. When the angel came down, what two things did he have?

_____

_____

2. How long is the devil to be bound?

_____

3. How many times in this twentieth chapter does it tell us how long Satan will be bound?

_____

_____

4. How many resurrections will there be?

_____

5. Do you believe that children will be born during the millennial reign and why?

_____

_____

_____

6. What will Satan's final end be?

_____

_____

_____

7. What was Origen's belief about sinners?

_____

_____

_____

8. What is the great white throne?

_____

_____

_____

9. What is the second death?

_____

_____

Chapter 21

Revelation 21:1-8

¹ And I saw a new heaven and a new earth: for the first heaven and the first earth were passed away; and there was no more sea.

² And I John saw the holy city, new Jerusalem, coming down from God out of heaven, prepared as a bride adorned for her husband.

³ And I heard a great voice out of heaven saying, Behold, the tabernacle of God is with men, and he will dwell with them, and they shall be his people, and God himself shall be with them, and be their God.

⁴ And God shall wipe away all tears from their eyes; and there shall be no more death, neither sorrow, nor crying, neither shall there be any more pain: for the former things are passed away.

⁵ And he that sat upon the throne said, Behold, I make all things new. And he said unto me, Write: for these words are true and faithful.

⁶ And he said unto me, It is done. I am Alpha and Omega, the beginning and the end. I will give unto him that is athirst of the fountain of the water of life freely.

⁷ He that overcometh shall inherit all things; and I will be

his God, and he shall be my son.
⁸ But the fearful, and unbelieving, and the abominable,
and murderers, and whoremongers, and sorcerers, and
idolaters, and all liars, shall have their part in the lake
which burneth with fire and brimstone: which is the
second death.

In this first verse John says, *"And I saw a new heaven and a new earth."* John also declares that the heaven and earth that we now live on and see around us (the sky) will be destroyed (or re-made) because of the sin that has polluted it. **It must be remade to be perfect, for God intends for the new heavens and the earth to be the home of all the saints of God, for God Himself shall dwell with them in the city of New Jerusalem.** Like many Bible scholars, I believe that this world was made over at least once before. I don't know what happened. Some believe that when Satan and his angels were cast out of heaven to earth, that they so polluted the earth, that God destroyed it. Peter tells us that the first heaven and earth *"which then was"* perished. It appears that this is a reference to the original creation in Genesis 1:1. And the second heaven and earth, *"which now are"* are kept in store, reserved unto fire. **After this, the new heaven and the new earth will come into being, the future home of God, Jesus, the Holy Ghost and all the saints of God.**

1 Peter 3:5-13

⁵ For after this manner in the old time the holy women al-so, who trusted in God, adorned themselves, being in sub-jection unto their own husbands:
⁶ Even as Sara obeyed Abraham, calling him lord: whose

*daughters ye are, as long as ye do well, and are not afraid
with any amazement.*

*⁷ Likewise, ye husbands, dwell with them according to
knowledge, giving honour unto the wife, as unto the weaker
vessel, and as being heirs together of the grace of life;
that your prayers be not hindered.*

*⁸ Finally, be ye all of one mind, having compassion one of
another, love as brethren, be pitiful, be courteous:*

*⁹ Not rendering evil for evil, or railing for railing: but contrariwise
blessing; knowing that ye are thereunto called,
that ye should inherit a blessing.*

*¹⁰ For he that will love life, and see good days, let him refrain
his tongue from evil, and his lips that they speak no
guile:*

*¹¹ Let him eschew evil, and do good; let him seek peace,
and ensue it.*

*¹² For the eyes of the Lord are over the righteous, and his
ears are open unto their prayers: but the face of the Lord
is against them that do evil.*

*¹³ And who is he that will harm you, if ye be followers of
that which is good?*

The new heaven and the new earth will be different than
the earth and heavens that we see around us and when we look
into the skies. This new earth, according to scripture, won't have
seas as the earth does today. **It will be an earth transformed,
prepared for the righteousness of God's holy city, the New Jerusalem,
where we will dwell with all the saints, with Jesus
and with God himself.** John speaks of the New Jerusalem as
"prepared as a bride adorned for her husband."

There sounded a great voice out of heaven, saying in

Verse 3, *"And I heard a great voice out of heaven saying, Behold, the tabernacle of God is with men, and he will dwell with them, and they shall be his people, and God himself shall be with them, and be their God."* As we look back to the beginning in Genesis, after God made Adam and Eve, He would come in the cool of the evening and walk and talk with Adam and Eve. **Mankind was created to have fellowship with God.** What the devil stole away, God is going to replace, and the saints of God will be with him throughout all eternity. He shall be with them and be their God. Scripture also tells us of our Savior's love and compassion for us. Verse 4 speaks of how **God shall wipe away all the tears** from our eyes, and there will be no more death; all sorrow will be lifted from our hearts. **There will be no crying, for there is nothing to cry about; all pain will cease, no pain to rake our bodies, and there will be no hurting. All these things will be taken away forever. Oh, how wonderful heaven will be!** We think of our loved ones who suffered so much before their death now alive, free of all sickness, all pain and all disabilities, and happy in the presence of our Lord. As we look back upon these scriptures, there are seven facts that we must not forget, that we must hold to:

1. That God shall dwell with man
2. That we, the saints, shall be God's people
3. That God himself shall be with us and be our God
4. That God shall wipe away all the tears from our eyes
5. That there shall be no more death
6. That there shall be no more sorrow or crying
7. That there shall be no more pain

We must remember these facts, for **all the former things have forever passed away, never to come against the children of**

242

God again.

John heard the voice of God telling him to write: *"Behold, I make all things new,"* for these words are true and faithful. In Verse 6, God spoke unto John and told him, *"It is done. I am Alpha and Omega, the beginning and the end."* The work that God was doing, the plan that God had made, was fulfilled, the work accomplished. God has the plan laid out, and the world is spinning according to His plan. The events that are happening are according to the plan. Nothing can stop this plan, but **we as the people of God can, by effectual prayer, change or slow down what God has set in motion in certain areas**. Noah changed God's mind about destroying man from the face of the earth, by serving God and living for him. By Abraham's prayer, Lot and his daughters were saved from destruction in Sodom. By Moses' prayer before God, **God spared the Hebrews and didn't destroy them because of sin. Again, we go back to the effectual fervent prayer of a righteous man that availeth much. God's plan is in effect, but if the church will bind together, we can touch God.** We need to be praying for one more great revival to reach the lost before it's too late, praying for God to deal with our families and loved ones one more time before Jesus comes. **We need to be under a burden for the lost, for if we don't pray for the lost, who's going to?** We cannot stop God's plan, but we can, by prayer, intercede in certain areas. Ezekiel 22:30-31 reminds us, *"And I sought for a man among them, that should make up the hedge, and stand in the gap before me for the land, that I should not destroy it: but I found none. Therefore have I poured out mine indignation upon them; I have consumed them with the fire of my wrath: their own way have I recompensed upon their heads, saith the Lord GOD."*

Here God tells us that He sought for a man to make up the

hedge to stand in the gap, and because He found none, His indignation was poured out upon the disobedient. **God is still looking for intercessors to stand in the gap, to pray for God's mercy upon the lost, to give them another chance.** If we say we love God and we do not love the sinner, then we lie. We must love the sinner; we must learn to separate the sinner from his sins. **We don't love the sin, we don't love the sinner's lifestyle, but we must love the sinner's soul. For before we were saved, all of us were sinners lost in sin.** But today we are no longer sinners. We are the saints of God, the redeemed, the blood bought; we are the bride waiting for the Bridegroom. In the last part of Verse 6, God tells us that He will freely give the water of life to anyone who thirsts.

Verse 7 tells us the promise of God is a promise that we must learn and lean on. *"He that overcometh shall inherit all things; and I will be his God, and he shall be my son."* This is our promise; it's up to us to live up to God's Word. Some will, but sadly, many will not. Who are those that won't enter into the kingdom of God?

When we begin to think about all who won't enter in, our hearts are made sad. One of the first things we must look at is the sins that condemn us. **Sin is the deeds which we commit that condemn us to a devil's hell.** There are those among us who believe that they can continue to commit the same deeds after they get saved that they did before they were saved, and there's no condemnation to them. I believe that if it's sin before we get saved, then it's still sin to us after we get saved. **If we live the same lifestyle and do the same things after we get saved, then what are we saved from?** Let us look at what the scripture tells us to be true.

Romans 1:22-32

22 Professing themselves to be wise, they became fools,

23 And changed the glory of the uncorruptible God into an image made like to corruptible man, and to birds, and fourfooted beasts, and creeping things.

24 Wherefore God also gave them up to uncleanness through the lusts of their own hearts, to dishonour their own bodies between themselves:

25 Who changed the truth of God into a lie, and worshipped and served the creature more than the Creator, who is blessed for ever. Amen.

26 For this cause God gave them up unto vile affections: for even their women did change the natural use into that which is against nature:

27 And likewise also the men, leaving the natural use of the woman, burned in their lust one toward another; men with men working that which is unseemly, and receiving in themselves that recompence of their error which was meet.

28 And even as they did not like to retain God in their knowledge, God gave them over to a reprobate mind, to do those things which are not convenient;

29 Being filled with all unrighteousness, fornication, wickedness, covetousness, maliciousness; full of envy, murder, debate, deceit, malignity; whisperers,

30 Backbiters, haters of God, despiteful, proud, boasters, inventors of evil things, disobedient to parents,

31 Without understanding, covenantbreakers, without natural affection, implacable, unmerciful:

32 Who knowing the judgment of God, that they which commit such things are worthy of death, not only do the same, but have pleasure in them that do them.

As we read these scriptures, we see a perfect picture of today's world. People are becoming vain in their imaginations, and their hearts are darkened. Professing themselves to be wise, they have foolishly turned their backs on God. **They worship the creature more than their creator. Their own lustful desires are more important than the things of God.** Romans 1:27-28 condemns the homosexual lifestyle that many are proudly living today, to their shame. In Verse 28, **God turns people over to a reprobate mind to do their own thing, to their shame and condemnation,** while Verses 29-32 lists more acts that are sin to people who do them. **These people, according to scripture, are worthy of death.** This doesn't mean that they should be killed; the death spoken of here is the second death, the final judgment of the soul, the casting of lost souls in the pits of hell (lake of fire).

1 Corinthians 6:9-10

> [9] *Know ye not that the unrighteous shall not inherit the kingdom of God? Be not deceived: neither fornicators, nor idolaters, nor adulterers, nor effeminate, nor abusers of themselves with mankind,*
> [10] *Nor thieves, nor covetous, nor drunkards,*
> *nor revilers, not extortioners, shall inherit the kingdom of God.*

These two scriptures again give us a list of sins that if committed by anyone (sinner or Christian) will keep them out of heaven. **Sin is sin regardless of who commits it, and unrepented sin will send the soul to an eternity without God.** Verse 9 tells us without any doubt that they who commit sin will not inherit the kingdom of God.

Ephesians 5:3-7

³ But fornication, and all uncleanness, or covetousness, let it not be once named among you, as becometh saints;
⁴ Neither filthiness, nor foolish talking, nor jesting, which are not convenient: but rather giving of thanks.
⁵ For this ye know, that no whoremonger, nor unclean person, nor covetous man, who is an idolater, hath any inheritance in the kingdom of Christ and of God.
⁶ Let no man deceive you with vain words: for because of these things cometh the wrath of God upon the children of disobedience.
⁷ Be not ye therefore partakers with them.

Again the Word tells us that **those who commit such acts and deeds will have no inheritance in the kingdom** of Christ and of God.

Galatians 5:19-21

¹⁹ Now the works of the flesh are manifest, which are these; Adultery, fornication, uncleanness, lasciviousness,
²⁰ Idolatry, witchcraft, hatred, variance, emulations, wrath, strife, seditions, heresies,
²¹ Envyings, murders, drunkenness, revellings, and such like: of the which I tell you before, as I have also told you in time past, that they which do such things shall not inherit the kingdom of God.

Verse 19 starts out by telling us that the works of the flesh are these. Then it proceeds to list what they are, although it doesn't give a complete listing. Not all these lists are the same; some list more sins than others. **But sin is still sin, and the reward for sin is death to the sinner or to the Christian who is not 100 percent sold out to God.** The backslider will go into hell alongside the unsaved. The only eternal security is to get saved and stay saved. To quote from Verse 21, *"as I have also told you in time past, that they which do such things shall not inherit the kingdom of God."*

Revelation 21:8

But the fearful, and unbelieving, and the abominable, and murderers, and whoremongers, and sorcerers, and idolaters, and all liars, shall have their part in the lake which burneth with fire and brimstone: which is the second death.

As we read Verse 8 again, we find still another list of those who will not be found in heaven. **God is surely trying to get the attention of wayward souls, those who shall have their part in the lake which burns with fire and brimstone.**

2 Peter 2:19-22

[19] While they promise them liberty, they themselves are the servants of corruption: for of whom a man is overcome, of the same is he brought in bondage.
[20] For if after they have escaped the pollutions of the world through the knowledge of the Lord and Saviour Jesus

Christ, they are again entangled therein, and overcome, the latter end is worse with them than the beginning.

²¹ For it had been better for them not to have known the way of righteousness, than, after they have known it, to turn from the holy commandment delivered unto them.

²² But it is happened unto them according to the true proverb, The dog is turned to his own vomit again; and the sow that was washed to her wallowing in the mire.

These verses are not written to the sinners of this world. **They are written to the church, the born-again believers, those who have gotten saved.** How do we know that they are saved? The Word tells us that they have escaped the pollutions of the world through the knowledge of the Lord and Savior Jesus Christ. This means only one thing, that they had a born-again experience with Jesus. After salvation, if we are again overcome, the latter end is worse than the beginning. **In other words, it would have been better for them to have never gotten saved than to get saved, backslide and return to the world.**

In these scriptures, one thing is perfectly clear. Those who indulge in these sins will not enter the kingdom of heaven. The list is long but points out the things we cannot do, if we are to make heaven our home. When the sinner accepts the Lord as his or her Savior, he or she must pray and seek the Lord for His divine help to overcome all of these sins. **When we get saved, our life instantly changes. When we are tempted, God gives us the power to say no to the devil.** There are those who will tell you that you must sin every day. Some do this to justify themselves, because they've never stopped doing the same old things; some because they don't understand the concept of sin. It's not a sin to be tempted, tested or tried. It only becomes sin when we yield to that temptation and partake of the sinful act. These six portions of scripture are very straight and to the point. Anyone who does these things will not enter the kingdom of God. Regardless of what people choose to believe, God's Word is the same yesterday, today and forever. It doesn't change. Sin will take the sinner to a very real devil's hell. When the scripture says that all liars will be in hell, it means ALL liars will be in hell. Maybe we should obey the scriptures we hear read at communion.

1 Corinthians 11:27-31

> *[27] Wherefore whosoever shall eat this bread, and drink this cup of the Lord, unworthily, shall be guilty of the body and blood of the Lord.*
> *[28] But let a man examine himself, and so let him eat of that bread, and drink of that cup.*
> *[29] For he that eateth and drinketh unworthily, eateth and drinketh damnation to himself, not discerning the Lord's body.*
> *[30] For this cause many are weak and sickly among you, and many sleep.*
> *[31] For if we would judge ourselves, we should not be judged.*

The scriptures tell us, *"But let a man examine himself."* **There needs to be self-examining taking place all the time through the Holy Ghost's anointing.** Remember the old saying: Sin will take you farther than you want to go; it will keep you longer than you want to stay; it will cost you more than you want to pay. **Sin is the destroyer of your soul. Those who think they can sin every day and still go to heaven are very, very wrong.**

If it's sin to do those things when you're lost, then it's a sin to do them when you claim to be a Christian.

2 Thessalonians 2:11-12

> *[11] And for this cause God shall send them strong delusion, that they should believe a lie:*
> *[12] That they all might be damned who believed not the truth, but had pleasure in unrighteousness.*

Ninety percent of the church will miss the rapture. Why? Because **they live under the delusion that once they are saved, they can continue to sin, with no fear of God bringing any judgment because they are saved.**

Part of the problem lies with preachers who are not concerned about their people. When we refuse to preach, teach and instruct people in the ways of God, we are held responsible. But **most of the fault lies with the people for not reading and studying for themselves what the Bible says**. There is no self-examining taking place today. There's so much that's not being preached or taught in our churches. God is asking why. What will our answer be on judgment day? We can't take man's word for anything when it comes to our souls. **Read the Word out of your Bible as the preacher reads from his.** The same with the Sunday school teacher and youth leaders. **Know that what they are reading is the true Word of God.** Read it for yourself every day and see how God will bless you. You will grow stronger in the Lord day by day and claim His blessings, for they belong to you as a born-again child of God. **His promises are for us. Use them, my brother or sister, and see what God can do and will do.**

Revelation 21:9-27

[9] *And there came unto me one of the seven angels which had the seven vials full of the seven last plagues, and talked with me, saying, Come hither, I will shew thee the bride, the Lamb's wife.*

[10] *And he carried me away in the spirit to a great and high mountain, and shewed me that great city, the holy Jerusalem, descending out of heaven from God,*

[11] *Having the glory of God: and her light was like unto a stone most precious, even like a jasper stone, clear as crystal;*

[12] *And had a wall great and high, and had twelve gates, and at the gates twelve angels, and names written thereon, which are the names of the twelve tribes of the children of Israel:*

[13] *On the east three gates; on the north three gates; on the south three gates; and on the west three gates.*

[14] *And the wall of the city had twelve foundations, and in them the names of the twelve apostles of the Lamb.*

[15] *And he that talked with me had a golden reed to measure the city, and the gates thereof, and the wall thereof.*

[16] *And the city lieth foursquare, and the length is as large as the breadth: and he measured the city with the reed, twelve thousand furlongs. The length and the breadth and the height of it are equal.*

[17] *And he measured the wall thereof, an hundred and forty and four cubits, according to the measure of a man, that is, of the angel.*

[18] *And the building of the wall of it was of jasper: and the city was pure gold, like unto clear glass.*

¹⁹ And the foundations of the wall of the city were garnished with all manner of precious stones. The first foundation was jasper; the second, sapphire; the third, a chalcedony; the fourth, an emerald;

²⁰ The fifth, sardonyx; the sixth, sardius; the seventh, chrysolite; the eighth, beryl; the ninth, a topaz; the tenth, a chrysoprasus; the eleventh, a jacinth; the twelfth, an amethyst.

²¹ And the twelve gates were twelve pearls; every several gate was of one pearl: and the street of the city was pure gold, as it were transparent glass.

²² And I saw no temple therein: for the Lord God Almighty and the Lamb are the temple of it.

²³ And the city had no need of the sun, neither of the moon, to shine in it: for the glory of God did lighten it, and the Lamb is the light thereof.

²⁴ And the nations of them which are saved shall walk in the light of it: and the kings of the earth do bring their glory and honour into it.

²⁵ And the gates of it shall not be shut at all by day: for there shall be no night there.

²⁶ And they shall bring the glory and honour of the nations into it.

²⁷ And there shall in no wise enter into it any thing that defileth, neither whatsoever worketh abomination, or maketh a lie: but they which are written in the Lamb's book of life.

These verses deal with the city of New Jerusalem. The angel tells John to come with him, and he will show John the bride, the Lamb's wife. John saw the city, the holy Jerusalem, coming down out of heaven. Verses 11-27 give us a description of what this city will be like. They tell us of the foundations, the walls, the gates and how big this city will be. Scripture states that the city will be four square. According to man's measurements the city was measured to be 12,000 furlongs or 1,500 miles square. There are some scholars such as Dakes and Larkin who believe that the city will be built in the shape of a pyramid. Other Bible scholars believe that the city will be in the shape of a cube. **When King Solomon built the temple, according to God's plans, which God gave to Kind David, in the building of the Holy of Holies, the place of the Ark of the Covenant, God's dwelling place, the room was a perfect cube.**

1 Kings 6:19-20

> [19] *And the oracle he prepared in the house within, to set there the ark of the covenant of the LORD.*
> [20] *And the oracle in the forepart was twenty cubits in length, and twenty cubits in breadth, and twenty cubits in the height thereof: and he overlaid it with pure gold; and so covered the altar which was of cedar.*

So, most Bible scholars believe that the New Jerusalem, since it is to be the dwelling place of God, and scripture describes a city built four square, will be in the shape of a cube. What do we know about this city?

1. There will be no temple – God and Jesus are the temple thereof.
2. The city will not have need of the sun – God is the light thereof.

254

3. The gates thereof shall never close; there will be no night.

4. Nothing that is profane, unwashed or that defiles can enter into God's holy city.

We will finally see Abraham's dream come true, for he looked for a city whose builder and maker is God.

Chapter 21 Review Questions

1. It was Peter's belief that the earth was created and de-stroyed, then remade into the world of today. Where are these scriptures found?

_____

_____

2. What was man created for?

_____

3. **There are seven facts that we must learn and not forget. What are they?**

      a. _____

      b. _____

      c. _____

      d. _____

      e. _____

      f. _____

      g. _____

4. What does God tell John in Verse 6?

_____

_____

5. Is it possible to change the mind of God?

_____

_____

6. Will the backslider go to hell? If yes, where is it found?

_____

_____

7. How big, according to man's measurement, will the city, New Jerusalem, be?

_____

_____

8. Can a person who sins every day go to heaven?

_____

_____

Chapter 22

Revelation 22:1-5

[1] And he shewed me a pure river of water of life, clear as crystal, proceeding out of the throne of God and of the Lamb.
[2] In the midst of the street of it, and on either side of the river, was there the tree of life, which bare twelve manner of fruits, and yielded her fruit every month: and the leaves of the tree were for the healing of the nations.
[3] And there shall be no more curse: but the throne of God and of the Lamb shall be in it; and his servants shall serve him:
[4] And they shall see his face; and his name shall be in their foreheads.
[5] And there shall be no night there; and they need no candle, neither light of the sun; for the Lord God giveth them light: and they shall reign for ever and ever.

In these first five verses, we still have a description of the city, New Jerusalem. **As we look at this holy city, we see that it's a perfect place prepared for a perfect people.** In Genesis, we read how God made man. When God finished, man was perfect. He lived in a perfect garden where there was no sickness or pain, because his body was perfect. Everything was great until sin entered on the scene. **Sin destroys everything it touches. But through the shed blood of Jesus Christ, we are brought back into a right relationship with God.** In Revelation, chapters 21-22, the Lord lets us know what lies in store for the born-again child of God. Won't it be wonderful there?

In Verse 1 it speaks of a pure river of water of life that will flow out of the throne of God and the Lamb. This river will flow in the midst of the street or wide boulevard that leads to the throne of God. Think how wide this street or avenue must be to have a river run down the middle of it. On both sides of this river grows the tree of life which produces twelve kinds of fruit, one for each month. **There will be no more curse of sin, for the throne of God and the Lamb will be there, and where God's throne is, there can be no sin.** We will be able to look upon God's face, and we will bear his name. In this city, there will be no night, for night will never come where God is. God will be the light of this city, and he shall reign forever and ever.

Revelation 22:6

And he said unto me, These sayings are faithful and true: and the Lord God of the holy prophets sent his angel to shew unto his servants the things which must shortly be done.

This is the starting verse of the conclusion of Revelation. The angel told John that all of these things are faithful and true, that the God of the holy prophets, through His angels, caused the prophets to testify of the things which must shortly come to pass, or be done. **We can rest assured that every prophecy that was given will come to pass, and most already have. The Word of God is the only absolute authority; there's nothing else in this world that is absolute, only God's Word.**

Revelation 22:7

Behold, I come quickly: blessed is he that keepeth the sayings of the prophecy of this book.

This verse starts with the word "Behold." **This word is used to get our attention, because what follows is very important and not to be missed. Jesus wants us to be aware that His coming is to be very soon.** The word quickly is used to emphasize how soon His coming will be.

Luke 21:26-28

26 Men's hearts failing them for fear, and for looking after those things which are coming on the earth: for the powers of heaven shall be shaken.
27 And then shall they see the Son of man coming in a cloud with power and great glory.
28 And when these things begin to come to pass, then look up, and lift up your heads; for your redemption draweth nigh.

Here we are told that when we see these things coming to pass, to lift up our heads for our redemption draweth nigh. We must, and again, we must be ready for the rapture (catching away) of the redeemed. The word tells us further that *"blessed is he that keepeth the sayings of the prophecy of this book."* **If we keep our lives clean of sin and follow God's Word, we will be blessed in all areas of our lives.**

Revelation 22:8-9

⁸ And I John saw these things, and heard them. And when I had heard and seen, I fell down to worship before the feet of the angel which shewed me these things.
⁹ Then saith he unto me, See thou do it not: for I am thy fellowservant, and of thy brethren the prophets, and of them which keep the sayings of this book: worship God.

John testifies that he heard and saw all these things, that it wasn't his imagination, but was the truth. As John realized the magnitude of what had transpired, he fell down at the feet of the angel to worship him. At this point the angel stopped John. He told John that he wasn't an angel, but was a fellow servant like John. **This man, whoever he was, was of the brethren of the prophets. I take it to mean that he was one of God's prophets who at one time walked this earth doing God's will.** His command to John was to worship God.

Revelation 22:10-11

¹⁰ And he saith unto me, Seal not the sayings of the prophecy of this book: for the time is at hand.
¹¹ He that is unjust, let him be unjust still: and he which is filthy, let him be filthy still: and he that is righteous, let him be righteous still: and he that is holy, let him be holy still.

In these scriptures, we see that John is told not to seal up the book. This is very important. In the book of Daniel, after his visions of these future events, Daniel is told to seal up the book; so why the difference? **The difference is that the coming of our Lord is so close that these warnings must be given out to the church and to all mankind.** The time is at hand, and we must prepare to meet the Lord. As we look at Verse 11, we see the finality of the warnings of this book. What do we mean by finality? This verse states to let man do what he will; let him be committed to his own lifestyle. If it's to do evil in the sight of God, so be it. If it's to do good and serve God, so be it. **The warning is given. We are responsible for where we will spend eternity.**

Revelation 22:12-19

[12] And, behold, I come quickly; and my reward is with me, to give every man according as his work shall be.
[13] I am Alpha and Omega, the beginning and the end, the first and the last.
[14] Blessed are they that do his commandments, that they may have right to the tree of life, and may enter in through the gates into the city.
[15] For without are dogs, and sorcerers, and whoremongers, and murderers, and idolaters, and whosoever loveth and maketh a lie.
[16] I Jesus have sent mine angel to testify unto you these things in the churches. I am the root and the offspring of David, and the bright and morning star.
[17] And the Spirit and the bride say, Come. And let him that heareth say, Come. And let him that is athirst come. And whosoever will, let him take the water of life freely.

¹⁸ For I testify unto every man that heareth the words of the prophecy of this book, If any man shall add unto these things, God shall add unto him the plagues that are written in this book:
¹⁹ And if any man shall take away from the words of the book of this prophecy, God shall take away his part out of the book of life, and out of the holy city, and from the things which are written in this book.

Beginning in this twelfth verse, our Lord again gives the warning, *"Behold, I come quickly."* Along with this warning, He informs us that His reward is with Him. He will give to every man according to his works. To emphasize His right to do this, He tells us who He is: *"I am Alpha and Omega, the beginning and the end, the first and the last."* Further, Jesus tells us that **blessed are they that keep His commandments, for they have the right to partake of the tree of life, and to enter into the holy city**. In the fifteenth verse are warnings to us to be very careful, for no sin can enter into the glory and presence of our God. Those who will miss out on heaven are considered dogs, sorcerers, whoremongers, murderers and idolaters, and whosoever loveth and maketh a lie.

Jesus again tells us who He is, and that He sent His angel to tell the churches the things which are to come. His right to do this is summed up in these words, *"I am the root and the offspring of David, and the bright and morning star."*

Verse 17 informs us that the cry of the church (the bride) and the cry of the Spirit is for Jesus to return. Let everyone cry out for the Lord to return. **The invitation is given again in the closing words of this book, for sinners and whosoever will, to come and partake of the waters of life freely.** Salvation is for whosoever will; all we must do is repent and accept Jesus as our

Savior. The world looks at the church as foolishness, that we believe in a pie in the sky. **But to us who have found peace in our hearts through our Lord Jesus Christ and salvation through His blood, our hope isn't in the things of the world which always fail; our hope is in God who never fails, who is eternal.** Paul said in Philippians 1:21, *"For to me to live is Christ, and to die is gain."* What Paul was saying is very clear, that as long as I live, Christ lives through me, to lead the lost to salvation. But when I die, I gain everything that I have preached about. I gain because I go to be with my Savior, my friend; I truly can go home to be with Jesus.

What do we want as Christian believers? Do we not want the same thing as Paul; do we not want the same thing as all who have gone on before us? Our heart's cry is to be with Jesus, to be truly in His presence, to hear Him say, "Welcome home, my child. Well done." As little children, we wanted the approval of our mothers and fathers. We wanted them to tell us that they loved us and to hold us close. Is this not what we want from Jesus and God our Father? **As I sit here writing these words, I feel an overwhelming desire to go and be with Jesus. As you read these words, I pray that you feel this same desire: to be with Jesus; to go home truly home to be with the Lord.**

Revelation 22:18-19

[18] For I testify unto every man that heareth the words of the prophecy of this book, If any man shall add unto these things, God shall add unto him the plagues that are written in this book:
[19] And if any man shall take away from the words of the book of this prophecy, God shall take away his part out of

the book of life, and out of the holy city, and from the things which are written in this book.

We read another warning that is given to men. The Lord knows our hearts, and He knows that man is corrupt without the saving power of God. **Man will take that which is holy and true and try to turn it to his own advantage, changing it to say what he wants it to say by whatever means he deems necessary.** A perfect example is the King James Bible. It was translated in the year of our Lord, 1611. It has been the mainstay of the church for over four hundred years. Multiplied millions of people have come to the Lord by and through the preaching of God's Word by this Bible. Now, in the last fifty to sixty years, the tried-and-true Bible, the King James, isn't good enough. Certain people have decided that they can do better, so they've changed the words, they've taken out the parts they don't like, and they've changed other parts to say what they want it to say. At the time of this writing there are 223 versions of the Bible on the market today according to the Internet. I personally will stay with the good old and well used (for 400 years), King James Version (KJV). The warning is clear: we are not to add to or take away anything from God's Word. **If we add to the Word, the plagues written in this book will be added to us. If we take anything away from this book, then we will be removed from God's book of life. The warning is plain; we cannot say that we didn't know. Each one of us will be held accountable for what we do; the decision is up to us.**

Revelation 22:20-21

²⁰ *He which testifieth these things saith, Surely I come*

quickly. Amen. Even so, come, Lord Jesus.
²¹ The grace of our Lord Jesus Christ be with you all.
Amen.

These last two verses give us the conclusion and the benediction of the book of Revelation and the whole Bible. Jesus testifies all these things, that they are true, and tells us one more time in warning: *"Surely I come quickly."* John adds: *"Amen"* and *"Even so, come, Lord Jesus."*

Then in Verse 21, John gives the benediction, the last prayer of the Book. *"The grace of our Lord Jesus Christ be with you all. Amen."* **Jesus has used His servant John to give to the church and to the world a vision of what the last days of the church and the world will be like. What we do with this information is up to us.** Some will never read it, because they don't believe in God. Some will read it, close the book, lay it aside and never do anything about it. Some will read it, take the words to heart and ask Jesus to save them from the wrath to come, and live for him and serve him. But the big question is what you will do about the words in the message that's in this Book.

Come quickly Lord Jesus. Amen.

Revelation 22:7

Behold, I come quickly: blessed is he that keepeth the sayings of the prophecy of this book.

Who is He coming after? **He's coming after those who keep the sayings of God's Holy Word.** God lays down the rules; the statutes are for us to live by. They are not grievous to those whose desire is to serve the Lord. To the world, God's laws mean nothing. The world lives by the devil's rules. Lying, cheating, stealing cursing, fornication, and such are all okay; just don't get caught. These people are not blessed of God and never will be. **The only way to be blessed of God is to serve Him with your whole heart, mind, and soul. Praise be to the name of God.**

This study is inspired by the Lord and is meant to be a blessing to you. I know we will not agree on everything. But there is one thing that we must agree on, and that is Jesus Christ's soon return for His bride. We, you and I, must be looking for His return if we are to make heaven our home. Remember, there is no sin found in heaven. We must be found living a life that is pleasing unto the Lord to make heaven our home. Remember the warning:

Behold I Come Quickly.

Chapter 22 Review Questions

1. Who shall reign forever and ever?

_____

_____

2. Who are these things shown to?

_____

3. What brings us back into a relationship with God?

_____

_____

4. Who is the only absolute authority?

_____

5. What words does Christ repeat so often in this chapter?

_____

_____

6. What is the cry of the Spirit and the bride?

_____

_____

7. How many versions of the Bible are there?

_____

_____

8. What does John add to Jesus' warning: "Surely I come

quickly?"

_____

_____

Bibliography

I would like to give my sincere thanks to the following writers who helped make this Bible Study on The Revelation of Jesus Christ possible. These writers have given me so much insight and knowledge. These authors were truly used of God; most have already gone home to be with the Lord. I can only say of them, that they left a wealth of knowledge behind. Now we as ministers and teachers need to use it, to build and strengthen the church of our precious Lord Jesus Christ. Thank you.

Brother Wilson

Rev. Matthew Henry
 Matthew Henry's Commentary on the Whole Bible
 Hendrickson Publishers Inc.
 Fifth printing – May 1998
 Copyright 1991

Rev. Albert Barnes
 Barnes' Notes on the New Testament
 Baker Book House Company
 Grand Rapids, Michigan
 Reprinted 2005
 Reprinted from the 1847 edition published by Blackie & Son, London

Rev. Finis Jennings Dake
 The Dake Annotated Reference Bible KJV
 Dake Bible Sales Inc.
 Lawrenceville, Georgia
 Twenty-seventh printing – April 1998
 Copyright 1963, 1991

Rev. Frank Thompson, D.D., Ph.D.
Thompson Chain Reference Bible KJV
B. B. Kirkbride Bible Co. Inc.
Indianapolis, Indiana
63rd printing
Copyright 1964

Rev. Warren W. Wiersbe
The Wiersbe Bible Commentary: New Testament
Published by David C. Cook
Colorado Springs, Colorado
Second Edition 2007

Rev. John Phillips
Exploring Revelation
The John Phillips Commentary Series
Kregel Publications
Grand Rapids, Michigan
Published 2001

Rev. Adam Clarke (1762 – 1832)
Adam Clarke's Commentary on the Bible
Abridged by Ralph Earle
Baker Book House
Grand Rapids, Michigan
Copyright 1967
Tenth printing – August 1977

Herbert Lockyer
All the Apostles of the Bible
Zondervan Publishing House
Grand Rapids, Michigan
Copyright 1972

All the Miracles of the Bible
Copyright 1961

Jay P. Green Sr.
General Editor and Translator
The Interlinear Bible
Hebrew, Greek, English
Sovereign Grace Publishers
Second Edition Copyrighted 1986

James Strong, S.T.D., L.L.D. (1822-1894)
Strong's Exhaustive Concordance of the Bible
King James Version
Abingdon, Madison, NJ
Copyright 1890
First edition – 1894   Thirty-ninth – 1980

John Gage Allee, Ph.D.
Webster's Dictionary
Designed for Home, School & Office
Harbor House Publishers Inc.

Rev Canon Leon Morris M.Sc., M.Th., Ph.D.
Introduction and Commentary on Revelation
Tyndale New Testament Commentaries
William B. Eerdman Publishing Company
Grand Rapids, Michigan
Sixth Printing 1978

William Barclay
The Revelation of John
The Daily Study Bible Series
Volumes 1 & 2
The Westminster Press
Philadelphia, Pennsylvania
Copyright 1976

J. Narver Gortner
> *Studies in Revelation*
> The Gospel Publishing House
> Springfield, Missouri
> Copyright 1949

Rev. Elizabeth Williams, D.D.
> *Prevision of History*
> Part One - The Book of Daniel
> Part Two - The Book of Revelation
> Messenger Publishing House
> Copyright 1974

Rev. Charles Spurgeon
> Sermon #1826 Preached at Metropolitan Tabernacle on 3/23/1884
> *The Horns of the Altar*
> The Spurgeon Archive
> http://www.spurgeon.org/sermons/1826.htm

Rev. J. C. Philpot
> A Sermon at Zoar Chapel, London, England
> Preached on 6/6/1841
> *The Sacrifice Bound to the Horns of the Altar*
> http://www.biblebb.com/files/philpot/sacrifice_bound.htm

Rev. Arthur Pink
> *The Antichrist*
> Internet Book
> http://www.pbministries.org/book/pink/Antichrist/anti_01.hm

Flavius Josephus (37 AD – 100 AD)
> *Josephus the Complete Works*
> Translated by William Whiston, A.M.

Kregel Publications
Grand Rapids, Michigan
Copyright 1960
Fourteenth printing 1977

W. E. Vine, M.A. (1873 – 1949)
Merrill F. Unger, Th.M., Th.D., Ph.D. (1909 – 1980)
William White Jr., Th.M., Ph.D.
    Vines Complete Expository Dictionary of Old and New Testament Words
    Thomas Nelson Publishers
    Nashville, Tennessee
    Published 1985
    Copyright 1984

J. D. Douglas, M.A., B.D., S.T.M., Ph.D.
    Organizing Editor of
    The New Bible Dictionary
    Wm. B. Eerdmans Publishing Co.
    Grand Rapids, Michigan

Rev. Eberhand Nestle
    Greek – English New Testament
    Greek Text – Literal Interlinear
    King James Version
    New International Version
    Christianity Today
    Washington, D.C.

Rev. Marvin R. Vincent, D.D.
    Vincent's Word Studies in the New Testament
    Hendrickson Publishers
    Peabody, Maine

Mark Water
Compiled by
The New Encyclopedia of Christian Martyrs
Baker Books
Grand Rapids, Michigan

Steve Gregg
Edited by
Revelation
Four Views a Parallel Commentary
Thomas Nelson Publishers
Nashville, Tennessee

Rev. Donald Grey Barnhouse
Revelation
An Expository Commentary
Zondervan Publishing House
Grand Rapids, Michigan
Copyright 1971

William Byron Forbush, D.D.
Edited by
Fox's Book of Martyrs
Zondervan Publishing House
Grand Rapids, Michigan
Copyright 1926, renewed 1954
Twelfth printing 1977

Webster's New World College Dictionary
IDG Books Worldwide Inc.
An International Data Group Company
Foster City, California
Fourth Edition
Copyright 2000

Test Your Knowledge Answers

Chapter 1 (page 23)

1. The Revelation of Jesus Christ
2. A Book of Warning
3. To the churches, and to the saints
4. Three
5. Isle called Patmos, for the Word of God and the testimony of Jesus Christ
6. To the seven churches in Asia
7. The Pastors
8. Ephesus, Smyrna, Pergamos, Thyatira, Sardis, Philadelphia, Laodicea
9. In the midst of the seven candlesticks

Chapter 2 (page 39)

1. Ephesus, Smyrna, Pergamos, Thyatira, Sardis, Philadelphia, Laodicea
2. The seven church ages
3. Thou hast left thy first love
4. To him that overcometh will I give to eat of the tree of life which is in the midst of the Paradise of God
5. He is the (first and the last, which was dead and is alive.)
6. He that overcometh shall not be hurt of the second death
7. Antipas was slain for standing up for the truth of God's Word and preaching it
8. He that overcometh and keepeth my work unto the end, to him will I give power over the Nations

Chapter 3 (page 55)

1. We can be alive in this natural body, but be spiritually dead at the same time; without the blood of Jesus to wash away or cover our sins, we are spiritually dead
2. The revival church
3. Yes
4. Behold I have set before thee an open door, and no man can shut it
5. The hour of temptation
6. The final end; there is no more
7. To see if they be of God
8. Through modernism and compromise with the world
9. Jesus is saying, I am knocking at your heart's door; if you will open it to me, I will come in and be your Savior

Chapter 4 (page 63)

1. A door was opened
2. In the first verse of Chapter 4 where the angel tells John to come up hither
3. Four and twenty or 24
4. They are:
   (a) The first beast was a lion
   (b) The second beast was like a calf
   (c) The third beast had the face of a man
   (d) The fourth beast was like a flying eagle
   (e) Each beast had six wings, and they were full of eyes.
5. The Holy Ghost

Chapter 5 (page 73)

1. The Word said that no man was able; that means no mortal man, but Jesus is more than man; he is the son of God
2. Because Jesus was born in the line and linage of David as prophesied
3. The prayers of the saints
4. The 7 horns represent the 7 spirits of God sent forth into the earth. The 7 spirits of God refer to the Holy Ghost fullness or completeness. The horns represent the power of the Holy Ghost. The eyes represent the all-seeing power of the Holy Ghost.
5. Because they contain the key to the rest of the book of Revelation. In Chapter 5, Christ is worshipped as our Redeemer.
6. (a) Be a near kinsman
   (b) By having the price to pay
   (c) Be willing to pay the price
7. Because they are collected and stored in gold vials. The scripture says "in vials full of odours," which are the prayers of the saints.

Chapter 6 (page 85)

1. The antichrist
2. To take peace from the earth
3. Scarcity and famine
4. Death and hell followed
5. Holiness and Righteousness of God
6. In the dens and rocks of the mountains

7. Poured out his vial upon the seat of the beast
8. The kingdom of the beast was full of darkness and they gnawed their tongues for pain, and blasphemed God because of their pain and sores but did not repent of their deeds.

Chapter 7 (page 95)

1. Events that do not happen in chronological order
2. To seal the servant of God in their Foreheads
3. 144,000 which is
4. 12,000 from each tribe
5. Raptured saints
6. Yes
7. No
8. Answers may vary

Chapter 8 (page 107)

1. About the space of half an hour (30 minutes)
2. Seven
3. Incense and the prayer of all the saints
4. One third of all the trees and all green grass
5. One third part of the sea
6. Wormwood
7. Woe, woe, woe, to the inhabiters (or the people who inhabit the earth) of the earth by reason of the other voices of the trumpet of the angels which are yet to sound

Chapter 9 (page 117)

1. The key to the bottomless pit

2. Locust, to torment man for five (5) months
3. Death
4. Hebrew = A-bad-don, Greek = A-pol-lu-on
5. From the four horns
6. An hour, and a day, and a month, and a year (13 months and 25 hours)
7. To slay the third part of man
8. Parenthetical
9. One third
10. Repent

Chapter 10 (page 123)

1. Jesus Christ
2. A little book
3. What the seven (7) thunders had said
4. To eat it
5. Prophesy again
6. Answers may vary

Chapter 11 (page 135)

1. Temple of God
2. It is given to the Gentiles
3. Enoch and Elijah
4. When the antichrist, the son of perdition, sets himself up in the temple of God and claims to be God
5. Come back to life and go back to heaven
6. Martyrs who gave their lives for God
7. The ark of his testament

Chapter 12 (page 147)

1. Parenthetical
2. Israel
3. Jesus Christ our Lord
4. Satan or the devil
5. One third
6. 1,260 days or 3.5 years
7. The devil cast out of his mouth water as a flood – meaning that the devil sent armies or soldiers after the Jews.
8. Numbers 16:26-34

Chapter 13 (page 157)

1. Literally, symbolically, figuratively
2. Masses of people; the antichrist will come from the people
3. Forty-two months (3.5 years)
4. Killed with the sword
5. The false prophet
6. Counterfeit
7. The image of the antichrist
8. In their right hand or forehead
9. Six Hundred Three Score and Six (666)

Chapter 14 (page 171)

1. Mount Sion
2. The hundred-forty and four thousand are Jewish saints
3. Parenthetical means events that do not take place in the order they are written

4. They are virgins
5. The warning is to not take the mark of the beast or to worship his image. To do so is to condemn one's self to eternity without God
6. There are three
7. Ten
8. a) The rapture of the church
   b) The battle of Armageddon at the end of the thousand years of peace

Chapter 15 (page 177)

1. Seven plagues
2. The hundred forty and four thousand (144,000) Jews
3. A vial
4. It is believed that the meaning of the smoke is symbolizing that the doors of mercy are closed and there is no more chance of salvation
5. Mankind was given direct access to the throne of God

Chapter 16 (page 187)

1. To go and pour out the vials of God's wrath upon the earth
2. There fell upon those who had the mark of the beast grievous sores
3. The seas will become as the blood of a dead man
4. Upon the rivers and the fountains of waters
5. Because they had shed the blood of the saints and the prophets
6. They work miracles to deceive the world and to bring them to battle

7. A plague of hail stones weighing about a Jewish talent or
   125 pounds

Chapter 17 (page 197)

1. The first woman called the great whore represents the
   apostate religion of the antichrist
2. Mystery, Babylon the Great, the Mother of Harlots and
   Abominations of the Earth
3. "I will tell thee the mystery of the woman and the beast"
4. It will be a world controlling government
5. Peoples, and multitudes, and nations, and tongues
6. The whore is the evil religious system
7. This evil religious system will be destroyed

Chapter 18 (page 209)

1. God is speaking to the Jews
2. 224 times
3. Rome
4. Because judgement/avengement has come
5. Imperial and Papal Rome

Chapter 19 (page 225)

1. The second coming is when Jesus comes back and sets his
   feet upon the earth
2. All born-again believers
3. Israel
4. Before the judgment seat of Christ
5. They are the Old Testament saints and the Tribulation

martyrs, who died in their faith
6. King of kings and Lord of lords
7. After the battle of Armageddon, those who are captured alive will be slain or killed
8. "and all the fowls were filled with their flesh"

Chapter 20 (page 237)

1. The key to the bottomless pit and a great chain
2. One thousand (1,000) years
3. Six times
4. Two
5. I believe there will not be any children born after the rapture because all innocence will leave the earth at the rapture, so why would God let more innocent people be born. What do you think?
6. He will be cast in the lake of fire
7. He believed that after death that sinners would be given a chance to repent
8. The Great White Throne is the final judgment throne
9. Being cast into the lake of fire

Chapter 21 (page 257)

1. 2 Peter 3:5-7
2. To have fellowship with God.
3. The seven facts are:
   a) That God shall dwell with man
   b) That we the saints shall be God's people
   c) That God Himself shall be with us and be our God
   d) That God shall wipe away all the tears from our eyes

e) That there shall be no more death

f) That there shall be no more sorrow or crying

g) That there shall be no more pain

4. It is done

5. YES, by effectual fervent prayer

6. YES, II Peter 2:19-22

7. 1,500 hundred miles square

8. NO, not according to scripture

Chapter 22 (page 269)

1. We, the saints of God, shall reign with Him forever and ever

2. John

3. Repent and accept Jesus as our Savior

4. The Word of God

5. I come quickly

6. Come (come Lord Jesus)

7. 223

8. Amen. Even so, come Lord Jesus

— Notes —

— Notes —

— Notes —

— Notes —

Jude

Verses 1-2

Jude 1:1-2

¹ Jude, the servant of Jesus Christ, and brother of James, to them that are sanctified by God the Father, and preserved in Jesus Christ, and called: ² Mercy unto you, and peace, and love, be multiplied.

Who is this Jude? Jude, Judas, or Judah, as he has been called, states that he is a servant of Jesus Christ. He also states that he is the brother of James (the Just) and the brother of Jesus.

Matthew 13:53-58

⁵³ And it came to pass, that when Jesus had finished these parables, he departed thence. ⁵⁴ And when he was come into his own country, he taught them in their synagogue, insomuch that they were astonished, and said, Whence

hath this man this wisdom, and these mighty works? ⁵⁵ Is *not this the carpenter's son? is not his mother called* *Mary? and his brethren, James, and Joses, and Simon,* *and Judas? ⁵⁶ And his sisters, are they not all with us?* *Whence then hath this man all these things? ⁵⁷ And they* *were offended in him. But Jesus said unto them, A prophet* *is not without honour, save in his own country, and in his* *own house.*
⁵⁸ *And he did not many mighty works there because of* *their unbelief.*

In Matthew 13:55, the brothers of Jesus are named; they are James, Joses, Simon, and Judas.

Mark 6:1-6

¹ And he went out from thence, and came into his own *country; and his disciples follow him. ² And when the sab-* *bath day was come, he began to teach in the synagogue:* *and many hearing him were astonished, saying, From* *whence hath this man these things? and what wisdom is* *this which is given unto him, that even such mighty works* *are wrought by his hands? ³ Is not this the carpenter, the* *son of Mary, the brother of James, and Joses, and of Juda,* *and Simon? and are not his sisters here with us? And they* *were offended at him. ⁴ But Jesus said unto them, A proph-* *et is not without honour, but in his own country, and* *among his own kin, and in his own house. ⁵ And he could* *there do no mighty work, save that he laid his hands upon* *a few sick folk, and healed them. ⁶ And he marvelled be-* *cause of their unbelief. And he went round about the vil-* *lages, teaching.*

Here in Mark 6:3, again the brothers of Jesus are named and they are James, Joses, Juda, and Simon. The scriptures also state that Jesus had sisters. Their names are not given, nor the number of them, but by simple deduction we know that there were at the least two, because scriptures states sisters. So, Jude was the brother of Jesus, our Lord.

In this epistle Jude doesn't claim importance as being the brother to Jesus, but with humbleness in his heart, his only claim is that he is the servant of Jesus Christ. I can understand the feeling that he must have had that he was not worthy to be called the brother of Jesus, and that his only desire was, "Just let me be your servant, Lord."

I believe as Jude was beginning to write this epistle, his mind went back to the days of his youth; the days also when Jesus began his ministry; the day when he and his brothers and sisters refused to believe that Jesus was the promised Messiah. Jesus even spoke of it in Mark.

Mark 6:4

But Jesus said unto them, A prophet is not without honour, but in his own country, and among his own kin, and in his own house.

Here Jesus admits that his family refused to believe in Him. They refused to accept Jesus because they, like all Israel, were looking for a great warrior king, a king who would come and once again make Israel a great nation. That wasn't the will of God for that time, though it will come in the future when Jesus returns. When did Jude repent and receive salvation? When did Jude accept Jesus as the promised Lord and Savior, the Messiah? We don't know.

The scripture does record that Jesus appeared to James

after the resurrection (I Corinthians 15:5-7). So it was shortly after this event, because the scripture tells us so. As we study the scripture, we find that Mary, the mother of Jesus, and Jesus' brothers were among the one hundred and twenty praying in the upper room when the Holy Ghost was poured out on the day of Pentecost.

Acts 1:13-14

> *[13] And when they were come in, they went up into an upper room, where abode both Peter, and James, and John, and Andrew, Philip, and Thomas, Bartholomew, and Matthew, James the son of Alphaeus, and Simon Zelotes, and Judas the brother of James.*
> *[14] These all continued with one accord in prayer and supplication, with the women, and Mary the mother of Jesus, and with his brethren.*

Jude does claim to be the brother of James. Some think this was to give his epistle more authority, since James was the head of the church in Jerusalem. Jude, like many of the other Apostles, worked in the background, where Paul, Peter, and others worked in the foreground. Jude did not seek self-glory, but only to please the Lord. For Jesus, himself, tells us that *"he that heareth his word and doeth it, is as his brother, and sister, and mother."*

Matthew 12:47-50

> *[47] Then one said unto him, Behold, thy mother and thy brethren stand without, desiring to speak with thee.*
> *[48] But he answered and said unto him that told him, Who is*

my mother? and who are my brethren?

⁴⁹ And he stretched forth his hand toward his disciples, and said, Behold my mother and my brethren!

⁵⁰ For whosoever shall do the will of my Father which is in heaven, the same is my brother, and sister, and mother.

We can have no greater witness than to have it said about us that we were humble servants of our Lord Jesus Christ. Jude directs this epistle: *"to them that are sanctified by God the Father, and preserved in Jesus Christ, and called:"*

Who are the called? The scripture states that many are called but few are chosen.

Matthew 20:16

So the last shall be first, and the first last: for many be called, but few chosen.

Matthew 22:14

For many are called, but few are chosen.

Who are the chosen? The chosen are all those who repent of their sins and accept Jesus Christ as their savior. God is not willing that any should perish but that all should have everlasting life. You say, "What's the catch?" There is no catch; the only requirement is that you, of your own free will, repent and accept Jesus as your savior. God will not make us do anything against our will; if we make heaven our home, it's because we chose to serve the Lord. If we make hell our home, it's solely because we chose to do so. God sends no one to hell; we send ourselves there, because of our own choices, actions, and desires.

I know that there are those who contend that we don't have a choice, but they are wrong. We are not put upon this earth with no choice as to our final outcome. Every one of us has the same opportunity; what we make of it is up to our own discretion. The Word tells that many are called, many are bid to the marriage. It is not God's will that any should perish, but that all should be saved. It's up to us; God will not make a man serve Him. If God forced us to serve, there would be no love. In the past some men and women were made slaves. Did they like their lives? Did they want to be slaves? The answer is no. They desired to be free to make their own decisions, to be their own person. God gives us this opportunity, the opportunity to decide, but we also must and have to reap the rewards of those decisions, be it good or be it bad.

Matthew 22:9

> *Go ye therefore into the highways, and as many as ye shall find, bid to the marriage.*

Romans 10:9-13

> *⁹ That if thou shalt confess with thy mouth the Lord Jesus, and shalt believe in thine heart that God hath raised him from the dead, thou shalt be saved.*
> *¹⁰ For with the heart man believeth unto righteousness; and with the mouth confession is made unto salvation.*
> *¹¹ For the scripture saith, Whosoever believeth on him shall not be ashamed.*
> *¹² For there is no difference between the Jew and the Greek: for the same Lord over all is rich unto all that call upon him.*
> *¹³ For whosoever shall call upon the name of the Lord shall be saved.*

1 Timothy 2:4

> *Who will have all men to be saved, and to come unto the*

knowledge of the truth.

Revelation 22:16-17

[16] I Jesus have sent mine angel to testify unto you these things in the churches. I am the root and the offspring of David, and the bright and morning star.
[17] And the Spirit and the bride say, Come. And let him that heareth say, Come. And let him that is athirst come. And whosoever will, let him take the water of life freely.

The summons (or call, or invitation) is given; what is your answer? I have heard all manner of reasons why people will not go to church and serve the Lord. The one used most is that the church is full of hypocrites, and I concede that this is true. But there is a judgment day coming very soon. So until that day comes, the wheat and the tares must grow together; just know that the harvest is near.

Matthew 13:24-30

[24] Another parable put he forth unto them, saying, The kingdom of heaven is likened unto a man which sowed good seed in his field:
[25] But while men slept, his enemy came and sowed tares among the wheat, and went his way.
[26] But when the blade was sprung up, and brought forth fruit, then appeared the tares also.
[27] So the servants of the householder came and said unto him, Sir, didst not thou sow good seed in thy field? from

whence then hath it tares?

28 He said unto them, An enemy hath done this. The serv-ants said unto him, Wilt thou then that we go and gather them up?

29 But he said, Nay; lest while ye gather up the tares, ye root up also the wheat with them.

30 Let both grow together until the harvest: and in the time of harvest I will say to the reapers, Gather ye together first the tares, and bind them in bundles to burn them: but gather the wheat into my barn.

The rapture of the saints is coming soon, but what of those who are left? Those who propose to live for God regardless of the cost that they have to pay, and there will be some. After the rapture has taken place the only way for them to enter heaven is to purpose to give their lives for the sake of God's kingdom. At the great white throne judgment there will be the final separating. The tares or sinners will be cast into the fire.

The biggest problem with the churches today is that the door to the world has been opened wide and the devil has walked right on in. The world is dictating what the morals and standards of the church are to be. When you make sinners feel comfortable in the church and there is no condemnation, no preaching of the true word of God. The church has failed, let's be truthful the church has backslid in favor of man's praise. The church is used to ease the conscience of ungodly men.

James 3:14-16

14 But if ye have bitter envying and strife in your hearts, glory not, and lie not against the truth.

15 This wisdom descendeth not from above, but is earthly,

sensual, devilish.

[16] For where envying and strife is, there is confusion and every evil work.

Jude, in this epistle, as we shall see, is giving a warning to not give heed to the many voices of the enemy. We are to be established in the Word of God, and not be led astray. James 3:14-16 tells us there should be no bitter envying and strife in our hearts, and that we are not to lie. But preachers and teachers get up and lie to people in every service in most churches today. This is the result of letting the world and governments dictate to the church of the living God, what morals and standards are acceptable to them. Whatever happened to letting God set the rules? It's a shame that people think they know more about what's morally acceptable than God's Word. James 3:15-16 states, *"This wisdom descendeth not from above, but is earthly, sensual, devilish. For where envying and strife is, there is confusion and every evil work."* There's enough evil in the world without the church being full of bitterness, envy, strife, and confusion, but it's here in our midst. The only way to get rid of it in our churches is to pray it out. Then preach the truth of God's Word. The truth will set us free.

John 8:23 says: *"And he said unto them, Ye are from beneath; I am from above: ye are of this world; I am not of this world."* To be sanctified by God, to be set apart from the world by the shed blood of Jesus Christ. We are to give ourselves to the service of Christ Jesus and God the Father, laying aside every weight and sin, living in the presence of God through Jesus Christ. In so doing, we are preserved unto God, and at the end of this life we will enter into the presence of God and into that place that Jesus has prepared for us, as he has promised.

www.ingramcontent.com/pod-product-compliance
Lightning Source LLC
Chambersburg PA
CBHW060251100426
42742CB00011B/1708